Dr. Swasawat,

Thank you for
your kind
encouragement.
All the best.

Kalakantha das
P.O. Box 247
La Crosse, FL
32658

BHAGAVAD
GITA

THE SONG DIVINE

A New, Easy-to-Understand Edition of
India's Timeless Masterpiece of Spiritual Wisdom

CARL E. WOODHAM

**TORCHLIGHT
PUBLISHING**

First printing 2000

Published simultaneously in the United States of America and Canada by Torchlight Publishing, Inc.

Library of Congress Cataloging-in-Publication Data

Bhagavad-gita. English.
   Bhagavad-gita: the song divine: a new, easy-to-understand edition of India's timeless masterpiece of spiritual wisdom / Carl E. Woodham.
   p. cm.
   ISBN 1-887089-26-8
I.Title: Song Divine. II. Woodham, Carl. III. Title.
BL1138.62 .E5 2000
294.5'92404521—dc2100-037730

Attention Colleges, Universities, Corporations, Associations, and Professional Organizations: *Bhagavad-gita: The Song Divine* is available at special discounts for bulk purchases for fund-raising or educational use. Special books, booklets, or excerpts can be created to suit your specific needs.

Printed in India by Ajanta Offset

For more information, contact the Publisher:

Torchlight Publishing
49334 Stagecoach Drive
Badger, CA 93603
Telephone: (559) 337-2200
Fax: (559) 337-2354
Email: Torchlight@spiralcomm.net
Web: www.Torchlight.com

BHAGAVAD

GITA

THE SONG DIVINE

Based on the *Bhagavad-gita As It Is*
by
His Divine Grace
A. C. Bhaktivedanta Swami Prabhupada

Rendered in English verse by Carl E. Woodham

Dedication

To Srila Prabhupada,
a pure devotee of Krishna,
whose *Bhagavad-gita As It Is*
and *Gitar Gan*
inspired this book.

Acknowledgements

I offer my respects and gratitude to Om Vishnupada Sri Srimad A.C.Bhaktivedanta Swami Prabhupada, whose *Bhagavad-gita As It Is* reveals Sri Krishna as the Supreme Personality of Godhead.

By good fortune Dr. Carl Herzig was in India in search of Vaishnava devotional poetry in English when we met. His expert editing as well as his gracious encouragement and guidance on this book were invaluable.

Bhurijana, Amala Bhakta, Saksi Gopal, Damodara, Keshihanta, Nagaraja, Dravida, Gaura-lila, and Mathuresh prabhus, all fine scholars of *Bhagavad-gita*, contributed in various ways to the composition of *The Song Divine*.

Advaita Chandra, Sujana, Kurma-rupa, and Padasevanam prabhus collaborated for the design and publication of *The Song Divine*. Thanks to them all for a job well done.

To my wife Jita and our children, K.C., Laxmi, and Leela, as well as to my parents, Ray and Marion Woodham and my sister Jan, my love and appreciation. Thank you for your support and encouragement during the years I worked on this book.

I am also indebted to Abhiram and Dhananjaya for encouraging the development of Vaishnava arts in general and *The Song Divine* in particular.

Contents

Foreword

The wisdom of the *Bhagavad-gita*, India's immortal spiritual classic, has illuminated that fabled land, from the Himalayas to the Ganges, since time immemorial. Gandhi read the book daily. And since it first became known outside India in the eighteenth century, it has inspired generations of philosophers, poets, and ordinary readers around the world. In America, Thoreau and Emerson sang its praises.

The subject matter of the Gita ranges from vast universal cosmology to our innermost life. We learn to see the world around us from the perspective of sages who saw the beauty of God reflected in every aspect of nature—the rivers, the mountains, the sky, the ocean, the plants, the animals. And we then learn how to move from appreciation of the reflected beauty of God to contemplation of the original beauty of God Himself. We learn that the journey of life did not begin with birth and will not end with the death of the body—for the soul there is neither birth nor death. We learn how we can become modern yogis, satisfied with the pleasure that comes from within, undisturbed by the turbulence of life in even the fastest lanes of third millenium society.

The most authoritative translation of recent years has now been rendered by Carl Woodham into verse of astonishing clarity, sensitive to the nuances of the original text as well as the tastes of modern readers, young and old alike. This invitingly accessible and lyrical volume is sure to win the hearts of all who value wisdom.

Carl Woodham brings to this refreshingly contemporary poetic rendition his own years of study and practice. He approaches the *Gita* as one who has endeavored to live his life according to its simple truths, who has discussed them endlessly with his wife, his children, and his friends. He is also a musician and singer, and these talents show through in this volume.

The Song Divine belongs on every seeker's bookshelf.

Michael A. Cremo
Co-author of *Forbidden Archeology:*
The Hidden History of the Human Race, and
Divine Nature: A Spiritual Perspective on the Environmental Crisis

Introduction

You have a message from Krishna.

Bhagavad-gita—the song (*gita*) of God (Bhagavan, or Krishna)—is Krishna's personal message to anyone interested in hearing it. Standing on an ancient battlefield, Krishna spoke *Bhagavad-gita* to the distressed warrior Arjuna. Krishna relieved Arjuna's anguish by explaining in exquisite detail God, the soul, and the relationship between the two. Today, *Bhagavad-gita* continues to enlighten, remove confusion, and strengthen resolve. Generations of readers have found it one of the most essential and succinct books of wisdom.

Krishna is the pivotal figure of the much longer *Mahabharata*, arguably India's greatest spiritual epic, wherein the *Bhagavad-gita* appears. Krishna's illuminating conversation with Arjuna forms the core of *Mahabharata's* teachings that has proven so inspiring to millions. Yet it's easy to overlook Krishna in the thicket of *Bhagavad-gita* translations. Most dismiss Krishna as a myth or a mouthpiece for some greater, formless Being. To do so is to miss the central point of the *Bhagavad-gita*: bhakti, or joyous, loving devotion to Krishna. The greatest luminaries of India's rich spiritual heritage, such as Ramanuja, Madhva, and Caitanya, have all drawn this devotional conclusion from *Bhagavad-gita*.

Almost thirty years ago, *Bhagavad-gita* primed my own spiritual quest and led me on a number of journeys to India. It seems that everyone in India knows *Bhagavad-gita*, but even there, Krishna's position often remains shrouded with cloudy interpretations. Although still just a polished novice, I feel fortunate to have encountered early on a *Bhagavad-gita* that pointed me directly to Krishna. That edition, *Bhagavad-gita As It Is* by Shrila A.C. Bhaktivedanta Swami Prabhupada, the world's foremost Vedic scholar and teacher of modern times, is the primary inspiration and source for *The Song Divine*.

With its clear, directly personal presentation of Krishna, *Bhagavad-gita As It Is* sweeps away the confusion that haunts most other editions. Take, for instance, text 9.34, where Krishna says: "Always think of Me. Become My devotee." One famous commentator explains the verse as follows: "It is not to Krishna we must surrender but to the unborn, unmanifest within Krishna." It takes a lot of mental gymnastics to interpret Krishna's statements that way, for in the brief course of the *Gita*, Krishna uses the Sanskrit words *aham* (I) and *mam* (Me) more than 100 times!

Precious few commentators give the person Krishna a benefit of a doubt when He makes such boldly monotheistic statements as, "I am the source of everything" (10.8), or, "Everything rests on Me as pearls rest on a thread." (7.7). What causes such reluctance to take Krishna's words at face value?

For one thing, the idea of God as a specific person tends to startle. It's safer to consider God at arm's length. In Civics class one reads abstract descriptions of the powers of the President of the United States in relation to the Cabinet, Congress, the military, and the Supreme Court. But if the

President knocks on your door, sits down on your couch and tells you about himself, your relationship with him suddenly becomes tangible—and personally challenging.

Some people may find Krishna hard to understand because they believe themselves to be God. Selling people on their Godhood undoubtedly makes good marketing sense, but it defies reason. If I'm God, why do my teeth ache? Why can't I stay young? Nonetheless, in their confusion some assert that *Bhagavad-gita* teaches that the soul and God are one. In fact, throughout *Bhagavad-gita* Krishna distinguishes the two but explains how the individual soul may choose to link with God in a loving relationship. The fruits of such a relationship— love, humility, compassion, steadiness—comprise a harvest far more valuable than a vague notion of Godhood.

In *Bhagavad-gita*'s twelfth chapter, Arjuna asks Krishna directly whether it is better to think of Him personally or in the abstract. Krishna replies that those who approach Him personally connect with Him most perfectly. He further explains that an abstract, formless conception allows one to progress, but only with *klesha*, much difficulty. Although *Bhagavad-gita* describes various spiritual paths, in this and many other passages Krishna emphasizes that the *most* confidential knowledge is to know and love God personally. After all, how deeply can one love or serve or talk to an abstraction?

Thinking of God as a person challenges our sense of human limitations. Everyone we meet is flawed. Is there really a person who is supremely wealthy, beautiful, strong, wise, famous, and yet detached? The Sanskrit word for such a person is *Bhagavan*, as in the title *Bhagavad-gita*. Setting aside any preconceived notions, the reader who at least theoretically understands

Krishna as *Bhagavan* opens the door to inspiration and enlightenment from *Bhagavad-gita*.

If we can hear from Krishna with humility and without depersonalizing Him, we have much to learn from *Bhagavad-gita*. At the same time, *Bhagavad-gita* does not direct us to join a particular religion or to leave home for a cave in the Himalayas. It simply advises us to turn to Krishna personally, now, in the heat of the battlefield of our lives.

Interpreting Krishna as mythical or impersonal drains the life-blood from the words of *Bhagavad-gita*, leaving the reader with a bowl of mystical mush. Following the lead of *Bhagavad-gita As It Is*, this edition lets Krishna speak for Himself. Lend an ear to Krishna and then, as He says at the conclusion of the text (18.63):

"Now I have explained to you the secrets of perfection.
Ponder to your heart's content, then act at your discretion."

Setting the Scene

These prior incidents from the *Mahabharata* help set the *Bhagavad-gita* in context.

Dhritarashtra and Pandu were brothers, princes, and heirs to the throne. Dhritarashtra, the eldest, had been born blind, so the huge kingdom went to the younger Pandu. Among the five sons of Pandu (known as the Pandavas), Arjuna was known as an incomparable warrior. Dhritarashtra had one hundred sons (known as the Kauravas), headed by the ambitious and evil Duryodhana.

Pandu died unexpectedly, leaving Dhritarashtra on the throne as caretaker for the young Pandavas. But Dhritarashtra's affection for his own sons clouded his judgement, leading him to acquiesce to Duryodhana's sinister attempts to kill the Pandavas. Duryodhana's attempts failed but ultimately led to a devastating war involving virtually all the major kingdoms of the earth.

Prior to the war, Krishna, king of Dwaraka, offered His vast army to one side and His personal services, in a non-combat role, to the other. The delighted Duryodhana assumed command of Krishna's army, while Arjuna felt equally pleased to have Krishna close at hand, humbly driving his chariot.

The battle between cousins is set to take place on the plain of Kurukshetra, north of present-day Delhi. The powerful sage Vyasadeva blessed Dhritarashtra's secretary, Sanjaya, with divine inner vision, enabling him to see the entire battlefield. Sanjaya thus reports on the events of the battle, beginning with this illuminating conversation between Arjuna and his chariot driver, Krishna—the *Bhagavad-gita*.

What's it all about?

Bhagavad-gita urges the reader to become a sage, in any external circumstance, by escaping the control of the three modes of material nature (goodness, passion and darkness). Under the influence of the three modes, the immortal soul becomes entangled in a temporary body and addicted to the fleeting pleasures of the physical senses.

One becomes a sage through *yoga*, or union with God. *Bhagavad-gita* divides yoga into three basic varieties: work *(karma-yoga)*, knowledge *(gyana-yoga)*, and devotion *(bhakti-*

yoga). In the first six of *Bhagavad-gita*'s eighteen chapters, Krishna describes how *karma-yoga*, work for God, leads one to *bhakti-yoga*, union with God through devotion. In the next six chapters, Krishna praises devotion *(bhakti)* and discloses His own divinity. In the final six chapters, Krishna explains detailed topics of spiritual technology *(gyana)*. He concludes that knowledge leads to devotion, and urges Arjuna to apply this conclusion in his own life.

Understanding the soul as distinct from the body makes yoga possible. Yoga means far more than the popular headstands and stretches commonly practiced as *hatha-yoga*. A true yogi, through loving service to God, rises above all external circumstances, even horrible situations such as Arjuna's— even death itself. To the enlightened sage, Krishna remains always accessible through yoga.

The Song Divine

In presenting *Bhagavad-gita* in English verse with brief comments on each chapter, I hope to make this great book easier for you to understand and enjoy. You'll encounter a few Sanskrit terms, explained in footnotes or in the prose summary following the poem. For simplicity's sake I left out many hard-to-pronounce names of heroes introduced in the *Mahabharata* but mentioned only briefly in the *Bhagavad-gita*. For similar reasons I also omitted a few cross-references to other Vedic texts mentioned in the *Gita*.

Despite the theme of simplicity, you will encounter several Sanskrit names for Krishna and Arjuna. I included these multiple names—with explanations in footnotes—to help maintain the color and flavor of the original text.

Virtually all Sanskrit literature is poetry. Here, rather than a strict literal translation, you'll find *Bhagavad-gita* in the classic and traditional English 'heroic couplets.' In converting the Sanskrit verses to English poetry, I have both lost certain nuances and invoked poetic license to add others. For instance, according to need, as is done in informal Sanskrit pronunciation, Arjuna is referred to as "Arjuna" (ar-JOON-ah) and at other points as "Arjun" (ar-JOON). For the sake of a more flowing English presentation, I have slightly rearranged the order of some verses. The chapter titles are loosely translated to clarify their content for the new reader.

In spite of my efforts to make it easy, some of the verses may still be hard to understand. A subsequent reading of Shrila Prabhupada's *Bhagavad-gita As It Is* will provide more clarification. *Bhagavad-gita As It Is* stands head and shoulders above the many other editions I've read. Through lauded by scholars, Shrila Prabhupada's word-for-word translations allow even a layman to peer into the direct, lyrical, and profound meaning of each Sanskrit phrase. His commentaries, revealing the personality of Krishna, allow one to capture the *Gita's* spirit and deeper meaning. With more than 40 million copies in print in all major languages, *Bhagavad-gita As It Is* has profoundly inspired far more readers than any other edition in history.

Krishna's instructions are found in *Bhagavad-gita*, while other Sanskrit texts, especially *Srimad Bhagavatam*, describe Krishna's activities. *Bhagavad-gita*, text 4.9, recommends understanding Krishna's activities as a means of liberation.

Shrila Prabhupada's elaborate translation of *Srimad Bhagavatam* or his summary study entitled *Krishna: The Supreme Personality of Godhead* make excellent follow-up reading to *Bhagavad-gita*. Also, for an authentic and enjoyable rendition of the fascinating events surrounding the *Bhagavad-gita*, read Krishna Dharma's condensed *Mahabharata*.

No poet, translator, or commentator can improve on Lord Krishna's own words. In *The Song Divine* I seek to bring the essential message of *Bhagavad-gita* to you lyrically but true to the original intent. From this edition you'll learn *Bhagavad-gita* in the ancient disciplic succession from Krishna Himself, represented in the modern world by Shrila Prabhupada, a fully self-realized spiritual master.

Srila Prabhupada's elaborate English translation takes several hours to read aloud. *The Song Divine* requires two hours. For a concise oral presentation of *Bhagavad-gita*, you'll find about 350 verses marked with special brackets ({1}) that can be read in less than an hour, yet give a good overview of the text.

The original *Bhagavad-gita*, an extemporaneous conversation conducted in fluent, ambrosial Sanskrit, passed in less than an hour. Yet for centuries, millions have repeatedly contemplated its words. Along with everything else, Krishna is also the ultimate poet. You're invited, through these verses, to become better acquainted with Krishna and His timeless, universal message.

Carl Woodham
Mayapur, West Bengal, India
December 19, 1999 (*Gita Jayanti* — the appearance day of the *Bhagavad-gita*)

1
Arjuna Gives Up

Dhritarashtra:

{1} What did my sons do at holy Kurukshetra plain?
Did they conquer Pandu's sons? Sanjaya, please explain.

Sanjaya:

{2} Listen now, O mighty king, as I disclose to you
Everything revealed within my heart by mystic view.
After your son Duryodhan surveyed the battlefield,
He bragged to guru Drona with his passions unconcealed.

{3-11} "All their mighty warriors," said your diplomatic son,
"Match the great Arjuna," and he named them, one by one.
"Yet," your son continued, "mighty Bhisma leads our clan.
Any of our generals can destroy them to the man!"

{12-13} The valiant Grandsire Bhisma, to inspire your son still more,
Raised a conchshell blast that sounded like a lion's roar.
Other Kuru soldiers, thus encouraged by your son,
Blew their conchshells loudly and beat fiercely on their drums.

{14-19} Standing on a chariot across the battle line,
Krishna and Arjuna blew their conchshells in reply.
Arjuna's four brothers, in a furious uproar,
Sounded sacred conchshells, and their captains added more.

Duryodhan and company, across the battleground,
Found their hearts were shattered by that pure and righteous sound.

{20-23} Banner flying Hanuman and arrows primed for war,
Arjuna surveyed the field and wished to see still more.
"Drive me, O Acyuta,"[1] said Arjuna to his friend.
"Take me to the enemies with whom I must contend."
"Let me see these warriors who have come here so inclined
To satisfy Duryodhan and his cruel, wicked mind."

{24-25} Then, before the deadly war, Lord Krishna, to comply,
Steered the splendid chariot between the warring sides.
Arjun's wise and mystic friend, engaged as charioteer,
Said to him, "Behold the many soldiers gathered here."

{26-27} Arjun saw on either side his family, friends, and guides
Clutching deadly weapons and prepared to fight and die.
Pained to see his relatives and friends in battle gear,
Arjun felt compassion and addressed his charioteer:

Arjuna:
{28-30} Seeing all my loved ones on this field prepared to die,
All my limbs are shaking and my mouth is going dry.
My Gandiva bow[2] keeps slipping through my trembling hand.
Skin ablaze and hair erect—I do not understand!
I cannot remain here, for my mind has gone to flight.
Only great misfortune can result from such a fight!

---

[1] "Acyuta" (A-chyoo-tah) is a name of Krishna meaning "infallible one."
[2] Arjuna won his famous Gandiva bow by pleasing Lord Siva.

{31-35} What will be the benefit of killing kin and friends?
Could I relish conquest of the kingdom without them?
What delight could life itself or any kingdom yield,
Killing those for whom we want such boons upon this field?
Grandfathers and fathers and the fathers of our wives,
Sons and even grandsons—here to win or give their lives!
Teachers, friends, and uncles watching me so viciously—
Why should I destroy them, even though they may kill me?
I won't fight for three worlds, let alone this single earth!
Dhritarashtra's sons will die! What would our joy be worth?

{36-38} Although they repress us, killing family is a sin.
What reward or happiness could I aspire to win?
Lesser, greedy men might kill their friends and family.
Why should we who see the sin destroy our dynasty?

{39-43} Breaking family lines means their traditions are destroyed,
Abandoning survivors to an irreligious void!
Sinful acts predominate and women are defiled,
Breeding unplanned children, undesired, running wild.
Outcast populations then create a hell for all,
Disrespecting ancestors and leaving them to fall.[3]
Actions done to break apart the family tradition
Stop all useful projects meant to help mankind's condition.
Krishna, I have heard from those who know these matters well:
Those who break up family lines will always go to hell.

---

[3] In the Vedic tradition, responsible family members offer food and water to deceased ancestors to assist their promotion in the afterlife. If such traditions are neglected, Arjuna fears the ancestors will suffer.

(44-45) How bizarre to find ourselves preparing for a sin!
Wanting royal happiness, we'd kill our very kin!
Let the evil sons of Dhritarashtra bring their arms.
Let them kill me now before I do them any harm!

Sanjaya:

(46) Brokenhearted Arjuna removed his arrow sheath,
Slumping on his chariot, his mind consumed with grief.

2

Reincarnation, Duty, and Yoga

Sanjaya:

{1} Shedding tears of pity sat Arjuna, quite depressed.
Seeing this, Lord Krishna made the following request:

Krishna:

{2-3} Tell Me why you give these unbefitting thoughts such worth,
Leading to dishonor and degraded future birth.
Don't give in to impotence with petty, weakened heart;
Rise, O mighty warrior—the battle soon will start!

Arjuna:

{4-8} Dear Krishna, how can I shoot my arrows in this fray
At Bhisma and at Drona, who are worthy of my praise?
I would rather beg than kill the elders of my clan.
They are wrong, but if I kill them, blood will stain my hands.
Even if I ruled the earth like demigods in heaven,
I could not shake off this grief which dries up my perception.
I don't know which way is best—to fight or to give in.
Dangerous as they are, I have no will to kill these men.
Weakness now confuses me. For truth, I turn to You.
I am Your disciple. Kindly tell me what to do.

Sanjaya:

{9-10} Having spoken clearly of his sorrow and his plight,
Arjuna said firmly, "O Krishna, I shall not fight."
As Arjuna sat between the armies, sad and weak,
Krishna simply smiled at him and then began to speak:

Krishna:

{11-15} Such a cultured speech, and yet your heart is filled with dread.
Learned persons never mourn the living or the dead.
Everyone has been alive throughout antiquity,
And never in the future shall we ever cease to be!
Bodies change from young to old. At death the soul must leave,
Taking a new body, as discerning souls perceive.
Winter turns to summer just as sorrow turns to bliss;
Sages remain steady through perceptions such as this.
One who learns to tolerate misfortune or elation
Surely becomes qualified for endless liberation.

{16-18} Studying both natures, seers of the truth proclaim:
Worldly things will always change, but spirit stays the same.
Spirit, which pervades the flesh, is permanent and whole.
Nobody is able to destroy the deathless soul.
Only outer bodies of the deathless soul must end—
Therefore, do not hesitate to fight, My learned friend.

{19-22} Thinking you can kill or can be killed are both in vain.
Spirit souls can never slay, nor ever are they slain.
How can one who knows the soul as indestructible
Think that he can kill someone or cause someone to kill?

You have not had birth or death all through your history.
You do not, you have not, and you will not come to be.
Constant and primeval, everlasting and unborn,
You continue living while your body's death is mourned.
As you put on fresh new clothes and take off those you've worn,
You'll replace your body with a fresh one, newly born.

23-25) Spirit can't be cut apart or burned by any blaze;
Water cannot soak it and no wind can make it fade.
Souls cannot be burned or dried or broken or dissolved.
Souls will never end or shrink or mutate or evolve.
Souls don't change. They can't be seen or mentally conceived.
Knowing this, the body's death gives you no cause to grieve.

26-30) If you think that death concludes the soul's manifestation,
Still you have no reason for this needless lamentation.
Every living body comes from worldly elements
And turns again to them at death. So why should you lament?
Souls cannot be slain, Arjun, by any man or thing.
Thus you need not sorrow over any living being.
Birth brings death, and after death, rebirth is imminent.
Duty stands before you, yet you sit here and lament!
Hearing of the soul amazes some who learn of it.
Others, even hearing, cannot understand a bit.

31-32) Fighting for religious cause—a warrior's obligation—
Is your highest duty. Stop this needless hesitation!
Happy are the warriors who receive the chance to fight,
Throwing wide for them the doors to heavenly delight.[1]

---

[1] According to the Vedas, the warrior who dies honorably in battle achieves a higher birth
in the heavenly planets.

{33-36} If you do not fight then sin will be your compensation.
Giving up your duty, you will lose your reputation.
People will speak ill of you; your name will be neglected.
Such a fate is worse than death, for you have been respected.
Many have considered you a warrior most empowered;
When you leave the battle, they will curse you as a coward.
Enemies will speak of you with impudence and scorn!
Such a fate would make you wish you never had been born.

{37} Either you'll be killed in war with heaven in your sight,
Or win an earthly kingdom, so get up, Arjun, and fight!

{38} Don't consider joy or pain or if you'll lose or win.
Fight for fighting's sake and you shall never incur sin.

39-40) I'll teach you to work with a detached mentality;
By such action you'll become perpetually free.
You shall waste no time if you endeavor in this way;
Just a little progress drives the greatest fear away.

41-46) Earnest souls take up this path with single-minded aim.
Those without detachment have a shifting mental frame.
In the jumbled minds of those attached materially,
Firm resolve to serve the Lord will never come to be.
Those possessing knowledge that is trivial and poor
Take the flowery Vedic words as heaven's open door.
Godly birth and wealth appear too tempting to ignore.
Wanting but a lavish life, they think of nothing more.[2]

---

[2] Here Krishna addresses Arjuna's earlier arguments. Although Arjuna's statements were
based on the Vedas, many people abuse the Vedas for materialistic purposes—such as a
heavenly birth—and thus miss their essential meaning.

Vedas deal with matter and its threefold qualities.
Rise above dull matter and have no anxieties.[3]
As a mighty reservoir replaces a small well
Higher Vedic teachings leave the lesser ones dispelled.

{47-48} Always do your work, Arjun, but do not claim its yield.
Neither think yourself in charge nor flee the battlefield.
Balanced in your duty, without care to win or lose,
Turn your work to yoga, as the learned sages do.

49-51) Stop all selfish actions and surrender to the Lord.
Only misers work with great attachment to reward.
Yogis rid themselves of work with good or bad reaction.
Strive, Arjun, for yoga, which is called the art of action.
Stopping work that leads them to be born repeatedly,
Yogis gain the highest state beyond all misery.

52-53) When you follow reason through the forest of delusion,
All you've learned or later learn will cause you no confusion.
Fancy Vedic words will no more agitate your mind;
You will always meditate in consciousness divine.

Arjuna:
{54} Dear Krishna, how does a realized soul behave and talk?
In transcendent consciousness, how does one sit or walk?

Krishna:
{55} Dear Arjuna, realized souls perceive themselves within;
Thus they can give up all petty, sense-indulgent whims.

---

[3] The three modes of material nature are goodness, passion, and ignorance. They control the unenlightened soul. Krishna describes them fully in chapters 14, 17 and 18.

56-57) Knowledge of the spirit, when completely understood,
Helps one become steady, whether times are bad or good.
Joy and sorrow never sway a steady-minded sage.
Sages are untroubled by attachment, fear, or rage.

{58-59} Sages draw their senses back from sight and sound and smell,
Just as cautious turtles draw their limbs within their shells.
Some repress the senses but desire still remains
Until there is a higher taste that leads them to refrain.

60-61) Senses are impetuous and forcibly take hold
Even of enlightened souls who try to keep control.
One who checks the senses with a mind absorbed in Me
Steadily progresses with the right mentality.

62-63) Dwelling on sense objects causes lust to catch on fire.
Lust produces anger, born of unfulfilled desire.
Anger breeds confusion and bewilders memory,
Causing lost intelligence and endless misery.

64-66) Free from love and hatred and from sensual addiction,
Sages gain the mercy of the Lord without restriction.
His profound compassion leaves a pleased and peaceful mind,
Miseries diminished, and intelligence refined.
Otherwise, the troubles of the mind will just increase.
How can you be happy when your mind is not at peace?

67-68) As a boat unanchored can be captured by the wind,
Even one unbridled sense can put you in a spin.

Anyone who curbs the endless cravings of each sense
Certainly becomes a soul of fixed intelligence.

(69) When the common man lies down, the learned souls arise.
When the common man wakes up, it's night-time for the wise.

(70) Mighty, endless rivers flow forever to the sea.
Seas accept the rivers without changing one degree.
Likewise does the river of desire never cease;
Learned souls observe desires, yet remain at peace.

71-72) Free of sense desires and the passion for acclaim,
Sages lead a humble life and never stake a claim.
Such devoted persons grow enlightened with each breath,
Reaching My supreme abode directly after death.

3
Karma-yoga: The Yoga of Action

Arjuna:

(1-2) Dear Krishna, by urging me into this ghastly war,
You appear to contradict what You have said before.
You said that intelligence is better, my dear Lord,
Than working with an aim for some material reward.

Krishna:

(3) Sinless one, some know the soul and thus are realized.
Others do their work for Me, as I shall summarize.

(4-8) Simply giving up your work will never set you free.
Mere renunciation won't fulfill you perfectly.
Everyone is helpless and is always forced to action,
Guided by the modes of nature and their interaction.
One who gives up sense objects but dwells on them within
Fools himself and acts renounced but really just pretends.
Rather than not working, you are better off to act.
Without work your very body cannot stay intact!
Work without attachment, with composed senses and mind,
Sages know as *karma-yoga*. That is more refined.

(9) Work performed as sacrifice, while living on this earth,
Must be done or you'll encounter further death and birth.

Simply do your duty so that God is satisfied;
That will keep the bondage of your karma set aside.

10-12) God created men and gods and gave them sacrifice,
Blessing them and saying, "This performance will suffice
To lead you to a happy life in full accommodation,
Placing you upon the sacred path of liberation."
Demigods take sacrifice and tend to human need.
Thus cooperating, man can prosper and succeed.
Demigods fulfill the needs of one with this belief.
One who won't reciprocate is certainly a thief.[1]

13) Devotees of God are liberated from all sin
Eating food first offered up in sacrifice to Him.
Others who prepare and eat their foodstuff at their whim,
Disregarding sacrifice, eat nothing more than sin.

14-16) Duty done as sacrifice will generate the rains,
Feeding everyone by growing life-sustaining grains.
Vedic scriptures therefore call for routine sacrifice.
Scriptures come from God, who manifests in His advice.
People who show disregard to Vedic regulations
Vainly spend their lives pursuing physical sensations.

17-19) Those who find the soul within, with depth of realization,
Take great joy and free themselves of earthly obligation.
Filling every purpose and completing every goal,
They depend on no one. Such is knowledge of the soul.

---

[1] In this section Krishna refers to Vedic ritualistic sacrifice for gods such as Indra, Siva, or Brahma. These rituals are performed for material gain, as opposed to service to Krishna, God, which is done selflessly to please Him.

Do your duty faithfully and think not of reward.
Work without attachment leads directly to the Lord.

{20-21} Janaka—the saintly king—by duty gained perfection;
You should do the same to give the common man direction.
Common men perform those deeds which great men introduce.
Great men set the standards which humanity pursues.

22-24) No work is required of Me, in planets low or high.
I've no needs, yet I discharge My duties as prescribed.
If I failed to do My work, because of My acclaim,
All the people of the world would surely do the same.
From this bad example, sinful actions would increase.
Unplanned population would destroy all earthly peace.

25-26) Foolish people, seeking gain, work hard all day and night.
Sages also work quite hard to set the people right.
Sages never stop the work of those who seek reward;
They instruct them how to work in service to the Lord.

27-29) Foolish people stay attached to sensual pursuit;
Sages leave them undisturbed and seek the Absolute.
Baffled by their egos, people think they can control
Actions that the modes of nature force upon their souls.
One who knows the Absolute and curbs his sense enjoyment
Knows that work performed for God is not mundane employment.

{30} Doing all your work for Me with vigorous delight,
Give up thoughts of selfishness, compose yourself, and fight.

31, 32) Faithful souls who do their work and seek My satisfaction,
Free themselves from envy and from past sinful reaction.
Others disregard My words and take their own direction.
33-35) Ignorance deludes them as they seek mundane perfection.

Yielding to their natures, even sages must pursue
Orders of the modes. What good will mere repression do?
Do not fill another's role, though done without a flaw;
Better that you do your work at risk of moral law.
Scattered in your path you'll find attachment and aversion.
Regulative principles protect you from diversion.[2]

Arjuna:
{36} Dear Krishna, what mighty force will not let one desist
From uninvited sinful acts, although one may resist?

Krishna:
{37} Dear Arjun, the lust of passion transforms into wrath,
Leading you upon an all-devouring sinful path.

{38} Like a fire concealed by smoke, a mirror thick with dust,
Or embryo within the womb, the soul is dressed in lust.

{39} Consciousness, by nature pure, grows covered with desire
That never can be satisfied and burns like blazing fire.

0-42) Lust resides within the mind, intelligence, and senses.
From it, one's bewilderment and ignorance commences.

---

[2] Regulative principles include Vedic injunctions to avoid flesh-eating, intoxication, non-procreative sex and gambling.

Senses govern matter and the mind controls each sense;
Soul surpasses all because it rules intelligence.
Knowing that the soul retains the ultimate position,
Set yourself to conquer lust—your deadly opposition.

{43} Arjuna, control this lust, the symbol of all sin.
Slay this foe of knowledge so real learning can begin!

Knowledge Through the Disciplic Line

Krishna:

{1-3} Long ago, when I created planets, stars, and sun,
I expounded yoga to the sun-god, Vivisvan.
He taught his son, Manu, mighty father of mankind,
Who taught his son Iksvaku, a renowned king of his time.
Saintly kings received My words in straight disciplic line,
Yet somehow this science has been lost in course of time.
Now, My friend and devotee, you too shall understand,
This ancient mystic knowledge of the link with God and man.[1]

Arjuna:

{4} Vivasvan was born long before You appeared, my Friend.
How did You instruct him at that time, as You contend?

Krishna:

{5} You and I, Parantapa,[2] have passed through many lives.
You do not remember, but My memory survives.

{6-9} As the Lord of everyone, My body is unborn.
Thus, in every age you'll see My transcendental form.
Any time or place that true religion starts to bend,
Irreligion rises, and at that time I descend.

---

[1] "Yoga" means literally to connect or link with God.
[2] A name of Arjuna meaning "conqueror of enemies."

Vanquishing each scoundrel and protecting every sage,
Reinstating righteousness, I come in every age.
One who knows the transcendental nature of My deeds
Takes no further birth, Arjun, but comes instead to Me.

10) Free of bondage, fear, and rage, within My custody,
Many sages past developed perfect love for Me.

(11) As one bows his head to Me, I bless accordingly.
Everyone, in all respects, is on the path to Me.

12) Worldly men serve demigods with sacrifice and praise.
Gaining quick results, they carry on their worldly ways.

13) Following their natures, people fall in four divisions.[3]
Though I made this system, people make their own decisions.

14-15) Work does not affect Me, for I have no aspiration.
Knowing Me this way helps you avoid all complications.
Knowing of My nature, all the liberated souls
Did their proper duties; you should emulate their goals.

16-18) Now I shall explain to you both action and inaction.
Even sages fail to know this to their satisfaction.
Action and inaction and those actions which are banned
Surely are quite intricate and hard to understand.

---

[3] Krishna refers here to the *varnashrama* social system, explained in detail in chapter 18, verses 41-44.

Wise and active persons can behold, with proper vision,
Action in inaction—and the opposite condition.[4]

19-21) Those whose every action is devoid of sense desire
Burn up all their karma in their wisdom's perfect fire.
Free of all attachment, though consistently engaged,
Working without karma in this ever-blissful stage,
People of such self-control take only what is needed.
Outcomes of their former sins are thoroughly completed.

22-24) Active transcendentalists are busy, yet remain
Steady and nonenvious, content with simple gain.
Rich in sacred knowledge, unattached and independent,
Actions of such persons merge completely in transcendence.
They seek only God's abode and act by His desire,
Actions then consumed by God like butter by a fire.[5]

5-29) Some yogis serve demigods by various oblations;
Some devote themselves to My Brahman manifestation.
Some submit their senses to the fire of restraint;
Others use sense objects with appropriate constraint.
Other seekers are more meditatively inclined,
Sacrificing senses in a calm and patient mind.
Some read through the Vedas and some give up all possessions;
Some use mystic yoga and still others try repression.

---

[4] "Action in inaction" means that the yogi is very dynamic within, something materialists do not understand. "Inaction in action" describes the yogis' external work, which is God-centered and creates no karma.

[5] In Vedic sacrifices, priests always offer pure butter (ghee) into a sacrificial fire. Similarly, unadulterated action for God becomes a sacrificial element in life. Krishna here explains that He accepts such actions as fully spiritual.

Others practice yoga to control their respiration,
Building up their life span to a very long duration.

30-32) All these different yogis gain a taste for sacrifice.
Purified in heart, they relish everlasting life.
Following your nature, choose among these applications.
Sanctioned by the Vedas, all are good for liberation.
In this world or in this life—or lifetimes subsequent—
Disregarding sacrifice, how *can* one be content?

{33-35} Transcendental knowledge is the consummate oblation.
Sacrifice in knowledge far exceeds renunciation.
Find a proper guru to inquire from and serve.
Realized souls impart to you the truth they have observed.[6]
Free from all illusion, you shall see the truth divine:
Every soul is but My part and thus is really Mine.

36-41) Using sacred knowledge as a boat of purity,
Former sinners cross an ocean full of misery.
Sin evaporates as sacred knowledge is acquired,
As a log is burned to ash when placed in blazing fire.
Transcendental knowledge proves incomparably sublime,
Dawning in the faithful yogis' heart in course of time.
Knowledge brings contentment to devoted, faithful souls
Seeking it persistently, with senses in control.
Yogis blessed with knowledge, who give up the fruits of action,
Realize the soul and rid themselves of past reactions.

---

[6] Here Krishna refers again to the chain of disciplic succession mentioned at the beginning of this chapter. A proper guru represents Krishna's original teachings as they are.

Foolish, faithless persons who deny the sacred texts
Can't achieve God consciousness in this life or the next.

{42} Slash your doubts of darkness with the weapons of the light.
Arm yourself with yoga and get up, Arjun, and fight!

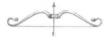

5
Acting in Consciousness of Krishna

Arjuna:

(1) Dear Krishna, please tell me clearly which is best to do:
Should I give up work, or should I simply work for You?

Krishna:

(2-7) Mighty-armed, both paths are good for gaining liberation,
But of the two, to work for Me transcends renunciation.
One who neither hates nor loves the fruits of his endeavor
Savors liberation from all worldly bonds, forever.
Detachment from matter and attachment unto Me
Are in fact identical, say those who truly see.
Thoughtful souls who serve Me come to Me without delay;
Others miss real happiness, renouncing work and play.
My servant is dear to all and to him all are dear.
His work brings no karma to distract or interfere.

(8-10) Yogis see and smell and hear; they act and never stall.
Yet within themselves they know they do nothing at all.
Though they speak or sleep or breathe, they always know the truth:
Senses deal with matter, while the spirit stays aloof.
One who serves the Lord and offers all rewards to Him,
Like a lotus leaf on water, stays untouched by sin.

11) Using body, senses, mind, and clear discrimination,
Yogis act exclusively for self-purification.

12) Steadily devoted souls gain undiluted peace
Rendering to Me the fruits of all activities.
Greedy souls ignore Me and pursue a selfish angle.
Coveting the fruits of work, they soon become entangled.

13-14) One who curbs his nature and whose greediness abates
Happily resides within the city of nine gates,[1]
Watching as the modes and their concomitant reactions
Bring about his work, its fruits, and other people's actions.

15) Baffled by desire, common souls find no accord.
Right or wrong, their choices are their own and not the Lord's.

16, 17) When one gains enlightenment, illusion is undone,
Just as darkness vanishes before the rising sun.
Wisdom, faith, and refuge take a single, Godly theme,
Leading one directly on the path to the Supreme.

18-21) Wise and humble sages see with vision, fair and equal,
Cows and dogs and elephants—and great or lowly people.
Those of equal vision, though residing on this earth,
Dwell in flawless spirit and transcend death and rebirth.
Tolerating pleasant things and things that bring them pain,
Knowing God and staying on the transcendental plane,

---

[1] The body with its two eyes, two ears, two nostrils, mouth, anus and genitals.

Such enlightened persons take no pleasure from the senses.
Focused on the Lord, their inner happiness commences.

22) Sensual enjoyment has a very short duration.
Sages do not relish it, avoiding tribulation.

23-26) Free your mind from doubt and keep it busy deep within.
Work for others' welfare and completely stop all sin.
Taming lust and anger and all other worldly urges,
Put up with this body—and tranquility emerges.
One whose joy is inward and is not materialistic
Reaches the Supreme and thus becomes a perfect mystic.
Free of want and anger, realized and self-controlled,
Liberated persons quickly gain the highest goal.

27, 28) Yogis shut out sense objects and take an inner vow,
Focusing their vision in between the two eyebrows.
Stilling in- and outward breath, restraining flesh and mind,
Fearlessly, they leave both lust and hatred far behind.

(29) Everything is Mine, Arjun. All work is meant for Me.
Know Me as your Friend and relish peace eternally.

6
Meditation and Mystic Yoga

Krishna:

{1-2} Son of Pandu, honest souls who work without desire
Mystically renounce this world, not they who light no fire. [1]
Reaching God in yoga is indeed renunciation;
Yoga practice means to give up sense gratification.

3-4) Neophytes should work at meditation to progress;
Elevated yogis put an end to worldly quests.

5-7) One must rise up with the mind and not degrade oneself.
The mind can be the soul's best friend—or make one's life a hell.
One who curbs the restless mind makes it his greatest friend.
Failing that, one's very mind torments him 'til the end.
Masters of the mind see God and gain tranquility,
Meeting joy and suffering with equanimity.

{8-9} Learned yogis feel content and keep themselves controlled,
Seeing things as equal, be they pebbles, stones, or gold.
One is even more advanced who welcomes equally
Total strangers, cherished friends, or even enemies.

---

[1] By "lighting no fire" Krishna refers to those who ignore their religious duties in the name of renunciation.

{10} Solitary, self-controlled, and through with mundane schemes,
Yogis use their bodies, minds, and souls for the Supreme.

{11-14} Seeking yoga, find a sacred place and go alone.
Lay out grass and deerskin cloth set not too high or low.
Seated firmly, mind absorbed in perfect concentration,
Purify your heart by doing mystic meditation.
Hold your head and neck and back in solid, upright pose,
Eyes in steady focus on the ending of your nose.
Mind subdued, devoid of fear and intimate relations,
Train yourself to think of Me within these limitations.

15) Curbing body, mind, and deeds with undeterred persistence,
Yogis go to My abode and end mundane existence.

{16-17} No one can do yoga if they fast or if they're stuffed,
Or if they sleep too much or if they do not sleep enough.
Moderating food and rest, as well as work and play,
Regulated yogis keep all miseries at bay.

18) Mind in perfect discipline and fixed in pure transcendence,
Able yogis trade their lust for inner independence.

19) Yogis contemplate the soul with mind always the same,
Just as lamps in windless places burn with steady flame.

20-23) Mundane mental actions thus entirely restrained,
Perfect yogis enter trance, as I shall now explain.
Purified, they see the soul and boundless joy commences,
Recognized and relished through their transcendental senses.

Fixed in bliss and resolute through any trial or pain,
Such enlightened yogis know there is no greater gain.

24-25) Deeply fixed in yoga with complete determination,
Use the mind to curb desire and all speculation.
Fixed upon the soul alone, with no mental affliction,
Step by step, one enters trance with wisdom and conviction.

(26) Fleeting and unsteady minds meander here and there.
Yogis must retrieve their minds and govern them with care.

27-28) Mind and passions set at ease, one feels great ecstasy.
Former sins give way to show one's true identity.

29-32) Yogis see all other souls with true equality,
Whether they are happy or awash in misery.
Yogis see Me in all souls and see all souls in Me.
I appear in everything enlightened yogis see.
One who sees Me everywhere, in everything that be,
Never loses sight of Me—nor is he lost to Me.
One who serves the Lord within—My own manifestation—
Certainly remains with Me in every situation.

Arjuna:
33-34) Dear Krishna, this yoga seems impossible to me!
Who can bear a restless mind that lacks stability?
Turbulent and stubborn minds do not want to give in.
Wouldn't it be easier to regulate the wind?

Krishna:

{35} Mighty son of Kunti,[2] though to curb the mind is hard,
You can meet your sense desires with full disregard.
Use your mind correctly and it soon shall be subdued.
Minds unchecked get in the way, according to My view.

Arjuna:

{37-39} Dear Krishna, suppose I start, but then I don't succeed.
What becomes of yogis who succumb to worldly needs?
Do they become drifting clouds who float from here to there,
All they have on earth and heaven vanished in the air?
Krishna, You and You alone can clear away this doubt.
I request You, Krishna, to completely drive it out.

Krishna:

{40-45} Dear Partha, a yogi's fate is always understood:
Evil cannot touch one who endeavors for the good!
Unsuccessful yogis, after years of godly bliss,
Reappear in rich families, or those of righteousness.
Sometimes fallen yogis reappear in future birth
As children of great yogis—rare indeed upon this earth!
Former yoga practice yields a forceful appetite,
Leading on to yoga, far beyond religious rites.
Thus endowed, in course of time, such yogis then proceed,
Pushing on with yoga 'til they finally succeed.

---

[2] Here Krishna prods Arjuna by referring to his royal heritage. Kunti, an illustrious princess, became the wife of King Pandu and the mother of Arjuna and his brothers. Another name of Kunti is Pritha, and thus Arjuna is also known as Partha, Pritha's son, as mentioned in verse 40 of this chapter.

Lifetime after lifetime, yogis purify the soul.
Reaching perfect yoga, they attain the highest goal.

46) Yoga is appropriate for any situation,
More than mere austerity or wealth or speculation.

(47) Of all yogis, one with faith who fixes Me in mind,
Intimately serving Me, affectionate and kind,
Though perceived by others as a low and simple minion,
Is indeed the greatest yogi. That is My opinion.

7
Absolute Knowledge

Krishna:

(1) Listen, dear Arjuna! You can ease your doubtful mind
Thinking of Me always as your knowledge is refined.

2) Take from Me all knowledge, both transcendent and mundane.
Doing so, no further need for knowledge shall remain.

(3) Of ten thousand people, hardly one will seek life's goal.
Of ten thousand seekers, hardly one knows Me in full.

4-6) Counting earth and water, I make matter of eight kinds:
Air and fire, reason, ego, ether, and the mind.
Moreover, My higher force consists of spirit souls
Tangled up in matter that they wish they could control.
Spirit enters matter, generating living beings.
I create all in this world, and I end everything.

(7) No truth lies beyond Myself, so do not be misled.
Everything depends on Me, as pearls rest on a thread.

{8-11} I'm the taste of water and I light the moon and sun.
I'm the sound of om[1] and the strength in everyone.

---

[1] Om or Omkara is the sound at the beginning of every Vedic hymn that addresses the Supreme Lord. Impersonalists, refusing to acknowledge Krishna's supremacy, do not utter His names but prefer to chant Om. Here Krishna says that Om also refers to Him.

I'm the fragrance of the earth, the heat of fiery blazes.
I'm the life of all that lives, the penance of the sages.
I'm the seed of everything; from Me all things arise.
I'm the great man's prowess and the wisdom of the wise.
I'm the vigor of the strong, yet I've no greed or lust.
Procreative acts are Me—when scriptural and just.

{12-14} Goodness, darkness, passion find in Me their very source.[2]
Thus, I'm independent and exempted from their force.
I am inexhaustible, the modes leave Me alone;
Others are deceived by them and thus, I am unknown.
Though the modes of nature are quite hard to overcome,
When you turn to Me, the modes will easily succumb.

{15} Four types count as pious and four other types do not.
Of the evil, there is one who won't give Me a thought.
One is called the lowest soul, possessed of shocking deeds.
Two others are wise and proud but godless in their creeds.

{16-18} Pious souls include the one who's suffering distress.
One is much in need of funds and hoping to be blessed.
One is very curious and puts Me to a test;
One who wisely serves Me, though, is certainly the best.
All these pious persons are undoubtedly great souls.
Still, of them, the wise shall ascertain the highest goal.

{19} After many births and deaths, those of discerning mind
Take Me as the source of all. Such souls are hard to find.

---

[2] Krishna here again refers to the three modes of nature, introduced in Chapter 2.

20-23) Those who misuse reason to materially acquire
Worship certain demigods to fill their own desire.
Sitting in their hearts, I help such souls become devoted—
Even faith misplaced will help the soul to be promoted.
People serve the demigods until their wealth has grown.
Anything they gain, in truth, has come from Me alone.
Some turn to the gods for wealth and notoriety.
My devotees conquer death and come to live with Me.

24-26) To those who ascribe Me to impersonal Brahman,
My eternal, perfect nature always stays withdrawn.
Though I am unborn and free of any imperfection,
Fools can never penetrate My curtain of deception.
I know all that came before, I know all things that be;
I know all things still to come, but no one can know Me.

27-28) Everyone is born into delusion and remains
Overwhelmed by hate and lust they simply can't restrain.
Souls possessed of piety, in this life and the last,
Worship Me, for all of their delusion has now passed.

29-30) Wholly rapt in spirit with each deed and thought, the wise
Shelter in My service from their aging and demise.
Knowing that I rule the world, the gods, and all oblations,
Sages reach Me after death in perfect realization.

8
Matter and Death, Soul and Supersoul

Árjuna:

{1-2} Tell me, Lord, what is Brahman? What is the world we see?
Clarify the soul, the gods, and karma, please, to me.
Who's the Lord of sacrifice? He lives within, but where?
How can I perceive You when I give up my life air?

Krishna:

{3-5} Souls are called Brahman, Arjun. Their nature is to serve.
Karma, or their actions, brings the bodies they deserve.
This world is but matter and it constantly transforms.
Demigods are parts of My vast universal form.
I'm the Lord of sacrifice, residing in each heart.
There, as Supersoul, I watch the soul, my tiny part.
If you die with mind on Me, unflinching and devout,
You will come to me at death. Of this there is no doubt.

{6-8} Any state of being one recalls when death prevails
Manifests again in his next lifetime, without fail.
Therefore, always think of Me, while fighting as decreed.
Work for Me and think of Me and to Me you'll proceed.
Meditate upon Me as the Personal Supreme,
Steadily, your mind immersed—and you shall be redeemed.

9) Think of the Supreme Person as one who knows all things,
He who is the oldest and controller of all beings.
Meditate on He who makes an atom seem immense,
He who bears the world and lies beyond all mundane sense,
Always as a Person, as resplendent as the sun,
Lighting up the darkness that envelops everyone.

10) One whose mind is focused as the time of death draws near,
So intent in yoga that no other thoughts appear,
Heeding the Supreme Person in absolute devotion,
Carries on to His abode, the ultimate promotion.

11-13) Vedic scholars utter "om" and enter the Brahman.
Hear about these celibates, and what they've undergone:
Closing all the senses' doors and focused on the heart,
Yogis raise the life air to the skull—and then depart.
Practicing such yoga, chanting "om" with thoughts on Me,
Potent mystic yogis journey straight to the Supreme.

(14-16) Yogis who remember Me, discarding other notions,
Come to Me more easily through service in devotion.
They shall not take birth again in fleeting worlds of pain.
No higher perfection waits for them to ascertain.
Birth and death rule all the worlds of demigods and men.
Come instead to My abode. You'll not take birth again.

17-20) Brahma's day, in human years, exceeds four thousand million.
Brahma's life, in human years, exceeds three hundred trillion.[1]

---

[1] Krishna here mentions Brahma, chief of the demigods, because he presides over one of the higher worlds mentioned in the previous verses. Krishna uses Brahma's life as an example of an enormous life span that, nonetheless, ends in death.

At his dawn, all souls obtain a body to possess.
At his dusk, all souls again become unmanifest.
All embodied souls appear with every breaking dawn;
Once again, at dusk, all souls are helplessly withdrawn.
Spiritual reality transcends this wheel of pain.
When this world exists no more, the spirit realm remains.

-22) From that realm I permeate and hold the whole creation.
Come there just by serving Me with utter dedication.
Sages call that destination flawless and complete.
Reaching My supreme abode, you never shall retreat.

-26) Mystic yogis leave this world by choice and not by fate.
Certain times are good to leave and others good to wait.
One may die, the *Vedas* say, in times of light or black.
Death in light means no more birth. In dark one must come back.
Those who know the Absolute depart when fire comes forth,
In the day, in waxing moon, and when the sun moves north.
Yogis who depart in smoke, at night, with waning moon,
Or when the sun is in the south return to earth quite soon.

27) Though devotees know these paths, their first priority
Is to stay absorbed in pure devotion unto Me.

28) Devotees retain the fruits of scriptural reflection,
Sacrifice, austerity, or giving up possessions.
Benefits of pious deeds are never lost to them.
More than this, they reach Me and do not take birth again.

9
God's Personality

Krishna:

{1-3} Dear Arjuna, since you have no envy toward Me
I'll present more wisdom to relieve your misery.
No instruction you could learn shall ever equal this
King of lessons, granting you direct, unending bliss.
Hear with faith, for faithless men do not achieve the goal.
Faithlessness brings birth and death, imprisoning the soul.

4-6} I extend, unmanifest, throughout totality.
Although I don't live in them, all beings live in Me.
Mighty winds blow everywhere and yet rest in the sky,
Just as souls move everywhere, while in Me they reside.
Though I maintain everyone and all the cosmic parts,
See how I am mystically aloof and stay apart!

7} Universes come from Me and end with Brahma's death.
Quickly, I create again, as one exhales a breath.

{8-9} I bid all to manifest and manifest again.
I bid all to be annihilated in the end.
While I am attending to destruction and creation
I stay unattached and keep a neutral situation.

{10-12} Though a tiny part of Me creates this cosmic storm,
Fools cannot detect Me when I come in human form.
Missing Me, such baffled souls pursue a godless route.
Without Me, their hopeful projects never quite work out.

{13-14} Great souls, on the other hand, know My divinity.
I protect them always as they lovingly serve Me.
Always chanting, always bowing, always finding ways,
Resolute devotees worship Me with love each day.

{15-16} Others seeking knowledge end up somewhat misinformed,
Taking Me as one, or all, or in My cosmic form.[1]
But it is I who am the chant, the ritual, the ghee.[2]
Fire, rite, and healing herb are just the same as Me.

{17-19} Universal father, mother, patriarch, and om;
Purity and Vedic knowledge—all are Me alone.
I sustain and shelter all. There is no better friend.
I'm the endless seed, both the beginning and the end.
I command the sky to clear and cause the clouds to swell.
Soul and matter come from Me, and life and death as well.

{20-24} Some research the *Vedas*, seeking heavenly employment.
Born on Indraloka,[3] they drink *soma*[4] for enjoyment.

---

[1] This verse refers to those who want to become one with God, those who worship everything as God, and those who worship the Lord's form as the cosmic creation as supreme. Chapter 11 addresses the subject of the Universal Form.
[2] Clarified butter, an essential part of any Vedic sacrifice.
[3] The heavenly planet of Indra, king of the demigods.
[4] A celestial beverage that prolongs life.

After lengthy pleasures, pious credits run their course,
Leaving Vedic scholars to take birth again by force.
Meaning but to worship Me, they chose a faulty creed.
My devotees never fall. I carry what they need.
Every gift and sacrifice is meant for Me alone.
Those who disregard Me can do nothing on their own.

25) Those who worship forefathers, the gods, or ghosts shall be
Born among such beings, but My servants come to Me.

{26-27} Cups of water make Me smile, though I could drink an ocean.
Fruits or flowers please Me, when presented in devotion.
All you do and all you give and all the food you savor
Offer first to Me with love and you shall win My favor.

28) Freed from both the good and bad results of your vocation,
Fixed on Me, you'll come to Me and gain your liberation.

{29-33} I've no partiality, no bias to transcend,
Yet by serving Me you shall become My trusted friend.
You may sometimes stumble, but don't let your heart grow faint.
When you resume My service I consider you a saint.
Endless peace and dignity you'll quickly realize.
Tell the world, Arjuna: My devotee never dies!
Man or woman, king or slave, I see with equal eye.
All who choose to come to Me shall never be denied.

{34} Be My servant. Think of Me. Bow down and take this boon:
Place your mind on Me alone and come to Me quite soon.

10
Seeing and Serving God

Krishna:

(1) Hear again, My dear Arjun, O man of mighty arms,
Knowledge that surpasses all I've said to you thus far.

(2-3) To the gods and sages, who themselves have come from Me.
My opulence and origin remain a mystery
I have no beginning and I rule all things that be.
Enlightened persons know this and become completely free.

(4-5) Learned people, free from doubt, of clear, straightforward mind;
Self-controlled and honest people, tolerant and kind;
Those rejoicing over birth or for whom death brings tears;
Peaceful, patient, fearless souls, or those beset with fears;
Tranquil, sober, generous souls, of fame or infamy,
All display an attribute supplied to them by Me.

(6) Seven saintly sages and the Manus and Kumars,[1]
I dispatched to populate the planets and the stars.

(7) One who knows My opulence and power without doubt
Links with Me in service, always steady and devout.

---

[1] All among the original descendants of Lord Brahma.

{8-11} Worlds of flesh and spirit both originate with Me.
Sages understand this well and serve me earnestly.
My devotees think of Me and serve Me all the time.
Speaking of Me makes their lives delightful and sublime.
Those who serve their Lord with love and do so constantly
Gain the understanding by which they can come to Me.
Showing them compassion, I, who dwell within their hearts,
Shine the lamp of knowledge and release them from the dark.

Arjuna:

{12-18} God of gods, Vyasadev,[2] and many other sages
Stated what You say and reconfirmed it through the ages.
You alone can know Yourself, for none can fathom You.
Tell me with Your pleasing words how I should think of You.

Krishna:

{19} Dear Arjun, though no one knows My fame to full extent,
I'll describe some features that I find most prominent.

{20-24} I'm the Supersoul, Arjun, Who dwells in every heart.
I'm the end of every being, its middle, and its start.
I am holy Visnu,[3] and of every sort of light
I'm the blazing sun of day; of stars, the moon at night.
Of the demigods I am the greatest you will find;
Indra, Siva, and Kuver.[4] Of senses, I'm the mind.
Himalayan mountains are, of solid things, like Me.
I'm the endless ocean and of plants, the banyan tree.[5]

---

[2] The compiler of the *Vedas*, who enabled Sanjaya to see all he is describing in the *Gita*.
[3] One of Krishna's expansions through whom He maintains the material creation.
[4] Indra is the king of heavenly planets; Siva is Krishna's partial expansion who presides over destruction; Kuver is known as the treasurer of the demigods.
[5] The vast banyan trees of India and other tropical places are among the largest living beings on earth.

{25-29} I am *om* among all sounds. The sacrificial call
Of My many holy names delights Me most of all.[6]
I'm Kandarpa, god of love, like Cupid with his bow.
I'm the cow Surabhi[7] who gives milk in endless flow.
I'm the thunderbolt of weapons, king among all men.
I am Yama, lord of death, who judges every sin.

{30-34} I'm Prahlad[8] of demon born, defected from his line.
I'm the lion among beasts. Of victors I am time.
I'm the Ganges, best among all rivers that flow by.
I'm the wind, the best among all things that purify.
I am everything, Arjun. Of science, I am proof:
Soul exists beyond the flesh. Of logic, I am truth.
I am "A" in alphabets, the shark among the fish.
I am Brahma, he who builds the world to suit My wish.
I am death, the end of all. I'm sire of all to be.
I am woman's patience, glory, speech, and memory.

{35-39} Of verses I am Gayatri.[9] Of seasons I am spring.
Of months I am November, time of peace and harvesting.
I'm adventure, victory, the splendor of the splendid.
I am gambling among frauds that cheat the ill-intended.
I am wisdom of the wise and strength among the strong.
I'm the staff of punishment that checks the lawless throng.

---

[6] Krishna has many, many names that are often chanted in mantra meditation, such as Hare Krishna Hare Krishna, Krishna Krishna Hare Hare/ Hare Rama Hare Rama, Rama Rama Hare Hare. See Appendix, Mantra Page.

[7] Surabhi cows are those that exist on the spiritual planets and are tended personally by Krishna Himself.

[8] Prahlad is the famous boy devotee whose father, Hiranyakasipu, was a powerful atheist.

[9] The sacred hymn chanted three times daily by *brahmanas*, or priests.

Life originates with Me. Of secrets I am silence.
Among men who seek to win, I am the moral science.

(40-41) There's no end, Parantapa, to My manifestations!
All that I have just declared is but an indication.
Know that every opulent and glorious creation
Springs but from a spark of My resplendent situation.

42) Dear Arjuna, why concern ourselves with many verses?
Just a tiny part of Me fills countless universes.

11
The Terrifying Cosmic Form of God

Arjuna:

{1-4} Dear Krishna, Your sacred words have caused my doubts to die.
Your perfection stirs my heart, O Lord of lotus eyes.
Though I love Your present form, the goal of meditation,
May I see Your giant form that fills the whole creation?
Can my mind conceive it? Will my senses still perform?
If so, then kindly show to me Your Universal Form.

Krishna:

{5-9} Dearest son of Pritha, now behold My mystic will:
Hosts of multi-colored forms and hosts upon them still!
Throngs of shining demigods step back to show you more,
Unveiling a vision no one else has seen before.
Anything you wish to see in any time or space
You can see completely, all at once and in one place.
Mortal eyes cannot perceive this endless form of Mine;
Therefore, I bestow on you the gift of eyes divine.

Sanjaya:[1]

{10-14} Then Arjuna saw a mass of faces, mouths, and eyes,
Bearing weapons, jewels, and clothes, unearthly in their size.

---

[1] In the oral version of this chapter, verses 11 and 12 are rephrased and spoken directly by Arjuna.

There in Krishna's body he could see the gods dispersed,
On countless stars and planets spread throughout the universe.
Many thousand blazing suns arising in the East
Couldn't match the radiance this cosmic form released!
Reeling in astonishment, his hair standing on end,
Arjun bowed and offered prayers before his mighty friend:

Arjuna:
{15-17} Gathered in Your body I see gods of awesome power:
Siva, sacred serpents, and Lord Brahma's lotus flower.
Bellies, arms, and eyes appear! I cannot comprehend!
Nowhere does it start, O Lord, and nowhere does it end!
Glowing clubs and discs and crowns have now surrounded me.
All the blazing glare has made it difficult to see!

{18-23} Krishna, You're the origin, the shelter of us all.
You're eternal truth, my Lord. You never slip or fall.
You see every secret with Your eyes, the moon and sun!
Flames shoot forward from Your mouth, consuming everyone!
Standing in one place, You stretch through stars and cosmic night.
All the worlds behold Your form and shrink away in fright!
Fearful gods bow down to You, and bow down yet again.
Perfect sages worship You by singing Vedic hymns.
Seeing this great form of Yours, with fearsome limbs and teeth,
All the gods are struck with awe! Like me, they seek relief.

{24-30} Multicolored hues in You extend throughout the sky!
I am filled with terror by Your gaping mouth and eyes!
Lord of lords, who holds the worlds, be gracious unto me.
I've become unbalanced as I see Your deathlike teeth!

Kuru warriors rush between Your giant, fearsome lips!
You devour limbs and skulls in bloody, grinding grip!
Like a river fills the sea or moths fly into fire,
People rush into Your mouth—the universal pyre!
Filling all the universe with dreadful, scorching rays,
You devour the multitudes who come from every way!

{31} I must know Your purpose, and I bow down in accord!
Tell me who You are, so fierce of form, O Lord of lords!

Krishna:

{32-33} Time I am, the death of all, and I am here to reign!
But for you, the Pandavas, all soldiers shall be slain.
Rise and fight and win your fame, and claim your right to rule!
Even now your foes are dead, and you are but My tool!

Arjuna:

{36-40} Perfect sages praise You, Lord, O conqueror of lust.
You alarm the evil but invigorate the just.
Primal Lord, the universe resides in You alone.
You fill every corner and You know all that is known.
You transcend this universe, which You alone create.
Who does not bow down to You, the greatest of the great?
You control the air and fire, the water and the moon.
Endlessly I bow and then again I bow to You.
I bow down from front and back. I bow from left and right.
Anything that's anywhere is but Your boundless might!

{41-44} You should thus be glorified by everyone who lives,
Yet I have made offenses I implore You to forgive.

Foolishly I spoke with You in friendly conversation,
Thinking You my equal as we sat in relaxation.
As a person overlooks a disrespectful friend,
As a lover disregards remarks that might offend,
As a father tolerates a coarse, unruly son,
Please excuse offensive things I've ignorantly done.

(45) Your gigantic form has left me paralyzed with fear.
Please again reveal Your form I've known for all these years.

Krishna:
(47-49) Dear Arjun, I've gladly shown this universal form,
Full of light and blazing mouths that none have seen before.
This has left you thunderstruck and filled your heart with fear.
Calmly now, behold Me in the way you hold most dear.

Arjuna:
(51) Chastiser of enemies, my fear has now declined.
Your enchanting human form at once relieves my mind.

Krishna:
(53-54) If you did austerities or gave your wealth away,
Still you could not see Me as you see Me here today.
Blessed souls who fill their lives with service done for Me,
See Me as I am, Arjun, and know My mystery.

55) One who acts with thoughts of Me and treats all as a friend,
Making Me the goal of life, achieves Me in the end.

12
Loving God

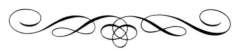

Arjuna:

{1} Tell me Lord, of these two paths, which one should I be on:
That of loving service, or the path to reach Brahman?
Some seek You impersonally and make Brahman their aim,
The all-pervading, changeless light that has no form or name.

Krishna

{2-7} Dear Arjun, the faithful soul who bows down at My feet,
Mind absorbed in Me alone, is surely most complete.
Formless meditation is quite troublesome, indeed!
Still, a sincere person may eventually succeed.
I shall swiftly rescue from the sea of birth and death,
Devotees who serve Me and chant My glories with each breath.

{8-12} Best to think of Me without a moment's deviation.
Next best is to practice *bhakti-yoga* regulations.
Bhakti-yoga teaches you to serve Me with affection.
Failing that, then work for Me and slowly reach perfection.
If you cannot work for Me in all of your concerns,
Do some work for charity, detached from what you earn.
Giving up attachment to the fruit of work, you'll find,
Far exceeds mere knowledge, for it brings you peace of mind.

{13-14} Devotees are kindly souls who act without false pride.
Whether times are good or bad, they're always satisfied.
Tolerant and self-controlled in peace or in disturbance,
They remain detached and stay determined in My service.

{15-17} Devotees cause no one else to feel anxiety,
Tolerating others, they are very dear to Me.
Devotees depend on Me and thus remain carefree.
Quite detached and expert, they are very dear to Me.
Devotees endure the urge to revel or to grieve.
Free of lust and sorrow, they are very dear to Me.

{18-20} One unchanged by praise or blame, the same in cold or heat,
Treating friend and foe alike, is very dear to Me.
One who gives up impure things, who's quiet and at peace,
Serving in each circumstance, is very dear to Me.
One who renders service in devotion, faithfully,
Making Me the goal of life, is very dear to Me.

13
The Field and Its Knower

Arjuna:

{1} Tell me of the soul and of the body that it owns.
What is their relationship? How is it to be known?

Krishna:

{2-4} Separating soul from flesh is knowledge well begun.
Sages say the body is the field, O Kunti's son.
Souls are called the knowers of the field in which they run;
Supersoul is He who knows the field of everyone.

{5-7} In *Vedanta-sutra*[1] the details are all revealed,
Telling of the soul within this body called the field.
It describes five elements and true and false conceptions,
Five senses that work for you and five that yield perception,[2]
Sense objects that lead the soul to lust and to despise,
Birth and growth and by-products and dwindling and demise,
Joy and pain all manifest—and then all put away;
Thus *Vedanta* tells of soul and field in interplay.

8-12) Now I shall explain to you what knowledge means to Me.
Wise and learned persons should acquire these qualities:

---

[1] *Vedanta-sutra* is a corollary Vedic text summarizing the philosophy of the *Vedas*.
[2] The five working senses include the arms, legs, voice, anus and genitals. The five senses of perception include the eyes, ears, nose, tongue and skin.

Humbleness, a lack of pride, a fondness for nonviolence,
Bowing to a guru who instructs you in this science,
Simplicity and tolerance, a taste for being clean,
Steadiness and self-control; a mind always serene,
Knowledge and detachment from the evils of this life,
Simple, peaceful life at home with husband or with wife,
Taking good and evil with an equal attitude,
Longing for a life alone in quiet solitude,
Honoring the value of the endless quest for truth—
Seek these forms of knowledge. From all else remain aloof.

13) Learn from Me of Supersoul and how the tiny souls
Think that they are of this world but stay in My control.

{14-19} Supersoul is everywhere. In every time and space,
He extends His hands and legs, His eyes and ears and face.
Giving you your senses, yet without senses Himself,
He's detached, yet cares for you and everybody else.
He lives in each creature, be it animal or plant.
You may try to see Him, but He's subtle, so you can't.
Like the sun, He's one, and yet He shines on every head.
When your body's born, He's there. He's present when it's dead.
He creates the brilliance of stars and moon and sun.
Learned persons see Him in the hearts of everyone.
Knowing Supersoul and how the flesh and soul entwine,
My devotees come to reach a nature more like Mine.

20-24) Worldly, changing matter is a nature of Mine, too.
Worldly joys and sorrows, though, are brought about by you.

You indulge your senses as they wander every day.
Matter, by My order, plays the game you wish to play.
As you turn to matter you will taste both joy and grief,
Traveling through lifetimes as a man or plant or beast.
In your heart, the Supersoul, the master watching you,
Permits you to follow what your senses say to do.
One who grasps this system of the soul enmeshed in pain
Finishes the present life and won't take birth again.

(25-26) Some will find the Supersoul by careful meditation,
Some by stopping selfish work, and some by education.
Others of more humble mind will simply worship Him.
Tending as they do to hear from sages, they transcend.

27-29) Those who see the Supersoul within and all around
Move ahead and don't allow their minds to drag them down.
One who sees the Supersoul, with soul as company,
In a frail and passing frame, is said to truly see.
Know that everything that moves or sits immovable
Is a spirit soul encased in matter dead and dull.

30-34) When you look no longer upon others as their flesh,
Seeing souls in everyone, your spirit is refreshed.
Those who see the body act as if seen from afar
See the soul within at rest and see things as they are.
Standpoints of eternity endow you with this view:
Though it meets with mortal frame, the soul remains unmoved.
Spirit soul pervades the flesh and yet does not dwell there,
Just as air that's mixed with all continues to be air.

As the sun illuminates the dark of outer space,
Spirit soul pervades the flesh while sitting in one place.

35) If you know the body as distinguished from the soul,
You can separate the two and reach the highest goal.

14
Surpassing the Three Modes

Krishna:

(1) Dear Arjun, now listen as I give you more direction,
By which many sages have attained supreme perfection.

2) That perfection means to have a nature more like Mine.
Once you have this knowledge, you leave birth and death behind.

3-4) Lifeless matter springs to life when I implant the seed.
Every species needs the soul in order to proceed.

(5-8) Matter comes in qualities of good and dark and passion.
These three modes induce the soul to act in different fashions.
Sinless one, the quality of goodness is most pure;
Goodness makes the soul feel light, contented and secure.
Passion is the quality created by desire.
Passion fills the souls with lust and cravings to acquire.
Darkness is the mode produced from ignorance most deep.
Darkness drives the soul insane and leaves it fast asleep.

0-13) Nature's modes compel each act of truth or fear or greed.
Constantly, the three of them compete to take the lead.
Goodness makes you happy, but when passion rules, you crave.
Darkness reigning causes you to be illusion's slave.

14-15)Nature's modes direct you when your body drops and dies.
Death in goodness means a birth among the good and wise.
Death in passion means a birth in which your lust increases;
Death in darkness means to take a birth in lower species.

(16)Acts in goodness bring about a sense of feeling jolly.
Acts in passion bring distress. Dark acts bring but folly.

17)Truth springs from the good, while greed is cut from passion's cloth.
Darkness brings but fantasy and foolishness and sloth.

(18)Those in goodness go to heaven, those in dark to hell.
Those in passion stay right here, for this world suits them well.

(19)When you see the modes perform in everything you do,
Seeing Me above the modes, you'll rise above them, too.

20)When you transcend nature's modes, their pain and their distress,
You'll conclude your birth and death and taste real happiness.

Arjuna:
(21)Dear Prabhu,[1] how does a person rise above the modes?
How am I to recognize his qualities and codes?

Krishna:
(22-25)Those in knowledge never hate to see the modes attack.
When the modes withdraw, the learned never want them back.
Tranquil as the modes and their reactions all unfold,
Sages see with equal eye a stone or mud or gold.

---

[1] Master.

Caring not for praise nor condemnation for some sin,
Stopping selfish action, in due time the wise transcend.

{26-27} Serving Me with faith and love in every situation,
You'll at once transcend the modes and their contamination.
This eternal stage is free from good or bad reactions.
Know Me as the basis of such endless satisfaction.

15
Supreme Personal Yoga

Krishna:

{1-4} So that you can understand the *Vedas* perfectly,
Now I shall describe a most peculiar banyan tree,
Branches reaching down and roots extending in the air,
Leaves comprised of Vedic mantras sprouting everywhere.[1]
Goodness, dark, and passion feed this endless banyan tree.
Rooted deeply in the business of society,
No one knows just where it ends or where this great tree starts.
Twigs attract the senses and ensnare the careless heart.
This confusing banyan tree binds up the weary soul.
Free yourself and cut this tree and make Myself your goal.

{5-6} Free of lust and false prestige and false association;
Free of the duality of sadness and elation;
Understanding spirit with an endless fascination;
You shall come to My abode, the highest destination.
My abode requires no sun or electricity.
Going there, you shall not miss the mortal banyan tree.

{7-9} Foolish souls, My tiny parts, who choose to stay behind,
Struggle with attachment to their senses and their minds,

---

[1] This verse refers to specific Vedic mantras or hymns explaining how to achieve short-term material happiness.

Rolling on from birth to death and birth to death again,
Holding false conceptions as a scent flies on the wind,
Each new birth enlivens them with sensual delight,
Full of mortal taste and touch and smell and sound and sight.

{10} Fools can never see the soul or how its bodies change.
Truth is only visible to one whose eyes are trained.

11) Striving transcendentalists can see the soul won't die.
Those who lack this knowledge can see nothing, though they try.

{12} Scattering the darkness that encircles everyone,
I create the brilliant fire, the splendid moon and sun.

{13-14} I enter the planets so they float along in space.
I enter the moonlight to give vegetables their taste.
I become the life air as it enters and retreats,
Helping living entities digest the food they eat.

{15} Sitting in their hearts, I give enlightenment to all,
Causing them forgetfulness and helping them recall.
All the Vedic writings are compiled by Me alone;
Thus, I know the *Vedas*—and by them I can be known.

{16-19} Every living being stands in one of two positions:
Those with Me are faultless, while all others are conditioned.
God Himself, distinct from both, maintains the worlds of all.
He's the greatest Person and He never slips or falls.

As I stand beyond both the enlightened and conditioned,
Vedic scriptures praise Me in that absolute position.
Knowing Me as God and putting all your doubts away,
You'll know everything and satisfy Me every day.

20) I present this Vedic secret just for your reflection.
Understanding this, you shall be wise and know perfection.

16
The Divine and the Demoniac

Krishna:

[1-5] Dear Arjuna, godly souls possess these qualities:
Fearlessness, enlightenment, austere simplicity,
Self-control and sacrifice, a life of purity,
Study of the *Vedas* and a taste for charity,
Honesty, nonviolence, no anger without cause,
Calmness and detachment and distaste for finding flaws,
Gentleness and sympathy for other people's needs,
Modesty and vigor and indifference to greed,
Cleanliness and fortitude and fixed determination,
Mercy, and an absence of the lust for adoration.
These transcendent qualities promote one's liberation.
Son of Pandu, surely you possess these inclinations.

[6] Knowing the divine and of their goodness and their truth,
Now hear of the demonic and their atheistic view.

[7-10] They don't know what they should do or what they should avoid,
Leaving truth and cleanliness completely unemployed.
Thinking that this world is false, with no God in control,
They say life is meant for sex, for lust consumes their soul.
Following this train of thought, with all discretion lost,
Building deadly weapons, giving no regard to cost,

Demons vainly strut about in false conceit and pride,
Led to ruin the world by lust that's never satisfied.

{11-12} Grabbing cash by any means to gratify their senses,
They create a network of a million false pretenses.
Building up a culture meant to bring the senses pleasure,
They produce anxiety beyond all earthly measure.

{13-15} Demons think, "Today I'm rich, with lots of wealth in store.
My opponent's dead and soon I'll kill a dozen more.
I'm in charge and everything is meant for my delight.
Everything I do is always absolutely right.
Wealthy friends and relatives surround me, far and wide,
None of them as wealthy or as powerful as I.
Now I shall give charity and feed the wretched poor."
Thus the demon sinks into illusion, more and more.

16-18) Stagnant, vain, and impudent, neglecting regulations,
Demons fake some rituals to build their reputations.
Done by crazy demons full of anger, pride, and sin,
Such pretensions desecrate the Lord who dwells within.
Flustered by anxiety and lust they cannot quell,
Demons stay attached to sin and fall down into hell.

19-20) Envy-driven rascals who are lowest among men,
Taking birth in lower forms again and yet again,
They eat stool and beastly foods with relish and great taste,
Shutting down the road to Me, their human life a waste.

{21} Lust and greed and anger are the gateways to this hell.
Sane people give up these three and serve their spirits well.

22-24) One who shuts the gates of hell and works for realization
Step by step moves closer to the highest destination.
Those who shun the scriptures and act only on their whim
Remain broken, sorry souls with prospects very dim.
Learn to do your duty and let scriptures bring you light.
Act by their direction and you'll make your future bright.

17
Faith, Food, and Sacrifice

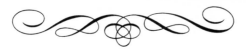

Arjuna:

1) What of those who don't use scripture for their information,
   Those who worship based only on their imagination?

Krishna:

2-4) Dear Arjun, the modes influence everybody's actions;
   Faith can also be in goodness, darkness, or in passion.
   Those in goodness serve the gods and all the godly host;
   Those in passion serve demons, and those in darkness, ghosts.

5-6) Foolish, godless penance born of greediness and pride
   Causes one to torture flesh and Supersoul inside.
   Disregarding scriptures and forsaking any reason,
   Such deluded worshippers are nothing more than demons.

7) Learn how nature's threefold modes pervade the food you eat
   And determine penance, sacrifice, and charity.

8-10) Foods in goodness please the heart and make you pure and strong.
   Juicy, fatty, wholesome foods bring health and make life long.
   Bitter, salty, pungent foods are dear to those in passion.
   Sour, dry, and burning fare brings negative reactions.

One in darkness chooses food that's rotten, stale, and old.
Putrid and untouchable, it's often eaten cold.

11-13) Sacrifices undergone as scriptures say they should,
By devoted, selfless souls, are always known as good.
Sacrifice performed in greed by persons who are vain,
Comes about from passion and is done for worldly gain.
Sacrifice in darkness means no foodstuffs are released.
Scriptures are neglected, leaving unrewarded priests.

14-17) Penance born of goodness takes in body, words, and mind.
Done for God, not profit, by the spiritually inclined.
Penance of the body means to bow to God and teacher,
Staying clean and celibate, at peace with every creature.
Penance of the speech means using words that don't disturb,
Referenced by the *Vedas* and intended just to serve.
Penance of the mind means taking simple gains and pleasures,
Making self-control and gravity your mental treasures.

18-19) Penance born of pride and done to gain respect and praise
Comes about from passion and will surely fall away.
Penance born of foolishness that aggravates one's flesh
Comes about from ignorance and causes much distress.

20-22) Charity in goodness should be given selflessly,
At the proper time and place, to one exemplary.
Charity in passion is just given for return,
Or given very grudgingly, without sincere concern.

Charity in ignorance is given out of place,
To unworthy people, and it always goes to waste.

23) Sages rise above the modes. God's pleasure is their theme.
Chanting "*om tat sat*,"[1] they sacrifice for the Supreme.

24-27) Undertaking sacrifice, penance, or charity,
Sages start with *om* as taught by scriptural decree.
Chanting *tat*, perform your sacrifice and charity,
Undertaking penance just to set your spirit free.
Sat means "the eternal," and such penance for the Lord,
Discharged for His pleasure, brings an absolute reward.

28) Sacrifice and charity the Lord does not accept
Sages call *asat*,[2] or useless, this life or the next.

---

[1] "That Supreme Eternal," indicating a sacrifice meant for spiritual advancement alone.
[2] Temporary.

18
Breaking the Bonds of Matter

Arjuna:

1) Hrishikesh,[1] what does it mean for one to be renounced?
What is the *sannyas*[2] order for whom it is pronounced?

Krishna:

2) Dear Arjun, a soul renounced gives up all trace of greed,
Shedding all attachment to the products of each deed.

(3) Some declare that any work will always have its fault.
Others claim that proper work will bring the right result.

(4) Best of men, now listen as I render My decision.
Scriptures say renunciation has its three divisions.

5) Never renounce penance, sacrifice, or charity.
Even sages do such things to build their purity.

6-11) To renounce in darkness means to fall into illusion,
Disregarding duty out of languor and confusion.
To renounce for fear of pain means doing so in passion.
Stopping work that's troublesome is simply mundane action.

---

[1] (Hree-shee-kashe) "Master of the Senses."
[2] *Sannyas* means "with nothing." Again, Arjuna is seeking clarification about acting with detachment without giving up his duty.

One in goodness always works because it is prescribed,
Giving up attachment to the fruits the work provides.
Giving service selflessly, without false expectation,
You shall know the meaning of complete renunciation.

12) Those renounced have no results to suffer or enjoy.
Others realize good and bad results they can't avoid.

13-16) Citing the *Vedanta*, I shall now explain to you
Five considerations that influence what you do:
One who acts, the body, all the senses, and the deed
And, of course, the Supersoul, determine what succeeds.
Right or wrong, all that you do with body, words, or mind
Comes about because of these five factors I've defined.
One who disregards these five and thinks himself in charge
Lacks the good intelligence to see things as they are.

17) One who fights and kills, Arjun, for duty, not for pride,
Keeps a clear intelligence and stays detached inside.

18-19) Knowledge, action, and the worker govern every deed.
Each has three varieties; now hear of them from Me.

20-22) Knowledge born of goodness lets you see each spirit soul
Linked with every other, yet distinct within the whole.
Knowledge born of passion makes all souls appear diverse,
Based upon their bodies, some as better, some as worse.
Knowledge born of darkness tends to be extremely small.
Missing truth, it makes one see one's work as all in all.

23-25) Action born of goodness is both regular and sane,
Void of love or hatred or an urge for selfish gain.
Action born of passion causes struggle and distress,
Done by persons lusty, proud, and eager for success.
Those who act in darkness disregard the scripture's words,
Unconcerned with bondage and distress it will incur.

26-28) Goodness blesses workers who have full determination,
Humble, pure, and eager in success or in frustration.
Workers steeped in passion are the pawns of joy and pain.
They are proud and greedy and will only work for gain.
Workers stuck in darkness tend to criticize and cheat,
Putting off their efforts while they catch a little sleep.

29) Listen to the ways the modes affect determination
And one's understanding as it suits each situation.

30-32) Goodness lets one understand and act with due concern,
Knowing what will free the soul or force it to return.
Passion in one's understanding makes distinctions blend;
Sin seems like religion and religion seems like sin.
Darkness in one's understanding makes good sense reverse,
Leading to decisions that will always make things worse.

3-35) One's determination is in goodness when it's firm.
Well-sustained by yoga, such a mind is hard to turn.
One's determination is in passion when it holds
To fruits of work and sacrifice with self-indulgent goals.

One's determination is in darkness when it stays
Wrapped in dreams and sorrow and a frightened mental haze.

36) Dear Arjun, now hear about the threefold happiness
By which people sometimes come to finish their distress.

(37-39) Happiness in goodness will enlighten from within.
First it seems like poison, but it's nectar in the end.
Happiness in passion tastes like nectar at the start.
Senses find it pleasing, but it leaves a poisoned heart.
Happiness in darkness is delusion all the way.
Born of sleep and laziness, it leaves the heart dismayed.

(40) No person, no demigod, no soul of any fashion,
Can resist the influence of goodness, dark, and passion.

(41) Nature forces everyone to work and to maintain
One of the four social orders I shall now explain.[3]

(42-45) *Brahmanas*, or wise men, tend to act with self-control.
Peacefulness and honesty surround these godly souls.
Ksatriyas, the warrior class, resourceful, firm, and stout,
Care for people's safety and keep adversaries out.
Vaisyas work the land and cows to earn and then invest.
Sudras are the laborers who humbly serve the rest.
Working by their nature, everybody can become
Perfect individuals. Now learn how this is done.

---

[3] This social system, known as *varnashrama dharma*, is meant to help every soul advance
spiritually according to their particular mode of nature.

46-49) Doing your own duty, you shall surely gain perfection
Serving the Supreme, who manifests in all directions.
Doing your own duty, though in need of some correction,
Supersedes another's duty done to full perfection.
Always do your work, Arjun, though flawed or unadmired.
Fault surrounds each action just as smoke surrounds a fire.
Checking all the senses and the urge for selfish action,
One renounces perfectly and ends sinful reaction.

50) Son of Kunti, learn from Me how you can realize
Transcendental knowledge, as I now shall summarize:

(51-53) Purified by wisdom, with your mind subdued and trained,
Freed from love and hatred, with your senses all restrained,
Living simply, eating little, words and mind controlled,
Practiced in renunciation, focused on the soul,
Free from quest for worldly goods, from ego, lust, and rage—
Thus at peace, you'll soon attain the fully-realized stage.

54-56) Joyful in transcendent bliss, released from tears and urges,
Equally disposed to all, at last you'll gain My service.
Service in devotion is the way to come to Me
And to live in My abode throughout eternity.
Though engaged in many ways, while under My protection,
Devotees go swiftly to that realm of sheer perfection.

7-60) Count on Me in every act and stay among My own.
In devoted service, keep your mind on Me alone.

Think of Me and I shall clear your obstacles away;
Acting out of ego, you shall never find your way.

61-62) If you fail to hear Me and defend the cause that's right,
Still you will do battle, for your nature is to fight.
I exist in every heart, directing every soul
Who inhabits vehicles of matter, dull and slow.
Bowing to Me utterly, in every way you know,
By My kindness you'll find peace and go to My abode.

(63-64) Now I have explained to you the secrets of perfection.
Ponder to your heart's content, then act at your discretion.
Since you're My beloved friend, I'll speak these final words,
Bringing greater benefit than all as yet you've heard:

(65-66) Think about Me always and become My devotee.
Worship and give homage and you shall return to Me.
Giving up religious creeds, submit yourself to Me.
I accept your former sins. Have no anxiety.

(67-69) Only speak these words of Mine to those who are austere.
Don't instruct those faithless souls too envious to hear.
If you simply teach My words among the devotees,
Your devotion is assured, and you'll return to Me.
Never in this world will any servant be more dear
Than the one who speaks My words and makes the meaning clear.

(70-71) I declare that one who learns this sacred conversation,
Worships Me with knowledge born of keen discrimination.

One who listens faithfully, with envy put aside,
Reaches higher planets where the sinless souls reside.

{72} Arjuna, with mind alert, have you now heard Me well?
Is your blind and dark illusion finally dispelled?

Arjuna:
{73} Infallible Krishna, my illusion is no more!
Taking Your instructions, I will surely win this war!

Sanjaya:
{74-77} Dear King Dhritarashtra, as I've made this presentation,
All my hairs have stood erect in spiritual elation!
In my heart I witnessed, by Vyasadeva's boon,
Krishna, Lord of mysticism, rectify Arjun.
Sir, as I again recall their sacred conversation,
I enjoy more pleasure and the thrill of inspiration!
Krishna's form repeatedly appears within my mind
Filling me with wonder and enjoyment every time!

{78} Where there is Lord Krishna, the supremely mystic Soul,
Where there is Arjuna, with his arrow and his bow,
Wondrous strength and wealth arise, and in their great profusion,
Righteous men shall win, O Master. That is my conclusion.

Chapter Summaries

Over thousands of years, *Bhagavad-gita* has inspired millions of people. Its powerful message of hope and enlightenment lifts the reader above the petty and temporal. The wisdom of the *Gita* leads to dimensions beyond ordinary education and enables one to analyze and understand life in a revolutionary way.

Bhagavad-gita means "the song [*Gita*] of God [*Bhagavan*]." Readers the world over consider the *Bhagavad-gita* the most important book of the Vedic literature—the vast body of ancient Sanskrit texts including and referring to the *Vedas*. The *Bhagavad-gita* is itself but one short chapter of the *Mahabharata*, a book so lengthy that Guinness calls it the world's longest. Yet in its short seven hundred verses, *Bhagavad-gita* distills the wisdom of all the *Vedas*.

To understand the *Bhagavad-gita* in context, consider these prior incidents from the *Mahabharata*: Dhritarashtra and Pandu were brothers, princes who were heirs to the throne. Dhritarashtra was born blind, and so the kingdom went to the younger Pandu. Pandu had five sons (known as the Pandavas), including the incomparable warrior Arjuna. Dhritarashtra had one hundred sons, headed by the ambitious and evil Duryodhana.

Pandu died unexpectedly, and Dhritarashtra accepted the throne as a caretaker for the young Pandavas. But Dhritarashtra's affection for his sons clouded his judgement, leading him to acquiesce to Duryodhana's sinister attempts to kill or vanquish the Pandavas. These attempts failed but ultimately led to a vast war involving virtually all the major kingdoms of the earth. The battle between cousins took place on the plain of Kurukshetra, north of present-day Delhi.

Chapter 1: Arjuna Gives Up

The *Bhagavad-gita* picks up the story with Dhritarashtra's inquiring about the battle from his secretary, Sanjaya. Through a special boon from the sage Vyasadeva, Sanjaya could see within himself all details of the battle. His vision includes Arjuna's hour-long conversation with Lord Krishna, Arjuna's charioteer, just before the war was to begin.

How has Lord Krishna, Himself a mighty king, assumed the menial duties of a charioteer? Before the battle, when both sides sought alliances, Krishna offered to send His vast armies to fight for one side, while serving personally in a non-combat role on the other. Duryodhana was delighted to have Krishna's armies, and Arjuna was equally pleased to have his dear friend Krishna with him on his chariot.

Sanjaya begins his narration of the battlefield scene by revealing Duryodhana's characteristic diplomacy and pride. After offering nominal praise to his opponents, Duryodhana loudly proclaims the superiority of his forces, the Kurus. The highly respected Bhisma—the grand-uncle of both the Kurus and the Pandavas—leads Duryodhana's army. But when the two sides raise threatening crashes of drums and conchshell blasts, it is Duryodhana's side that feels intimidated.

Arjuna is full of confidence, with the emblem of the heroic monkey warrior Hanuman on his chariot flag. Arjuna asks Lord Krishna to drive him between the two armies so he can study his opponents. When Arjuna fully realizes that the battle will result in the deaths of so many dear relatives, he suddenly loses his resolve to fight. In shock, he presents Lord Krishna with many good reasons why he has decided to walk away from the battle.

Chapter 2: Reincarnation, Duty, and Yoga

Krishna quickly rejects Arjuna's decision to refrain from battle. Arjuna admits he is confused and asks for instruction. In the remaining verses of this chapter—some of the most well known in the *Bhagavad-gita*—Krishna presents three reasons for Arjuna to change his mind:

1. The eternal soul, distinct from the temporary body, reincarnates through various lifetimes (verses 11-30).

2. As a warrior, Arjuna has a duty to fight (31-38).

3. Arjuna's reasons for not fighting, although having some basis in Vedic scripture, miss the higher purpose of the *Vedas*—specifically, to transcend material circumstance through yoga (39-53).

After Arjuna asks for clarification, Krishna concludes the chapter with a further explanation of yoga and transcendence.

The concept of yoga, introduced in this chapter, reappears throughout the rest of the *Bhagavad-gita*. Yoga is much more than the *hatha-yoga* exercises familiar in the West. Yoga, the root of the word yoke, means "to link" with God. In this chapter Lord Krishna presents the basics of yoga: control of the mind, control of the senses, and pursuit of happiness higher than what can be found through the mind and senses. In later chapters Krishna details various yoga paths.

We are also introduced in this chapter (verse 45) to the three modes of nature. These divisions or qualities of matter—goodness, passion, and ignorance—constitute one of Lord Krishna's most vivid teachings. As a painter mixes blue, red, and yellow to create the endless spectrum of colors, so nature combines goodness, passion, and ignorance to influence and create distinct qualities in everyone and everything. Later chapters describe the effects of the modes on aspects of life including food, work, education, and worship. Through yoga one clears away the influences of the modes.

In both Chapters One and Two we find references to "heaven," which refers not to the spiritual kingdom of God but to higher material planets, occupied by powerful *devas*, or gods. Since the gods enjoy long life and extensive pleasures, the *Vedas* offer interested humans various means to attain their heavenly worlds. Here in Chapter Two, for the first of many times in the *Bhagavad-gita*, Lord Krishna rejects such motivated and polytheistic worship as inferior and mundane.

Chapter 3: Karma-yoga: The Yoga of Action

Karma refers to moral action and reaction. According to the law of karma, whatever actions one performs bring reactions. Good karma might manifest as wealth, power, and prestige, while bad karma may appear as debt, disease, and vulnerability. Since the soul is eternal, as explained in Chapter

Two, it carries karmic reactions from one life to the next. Karma entangles the soul in material activities and ignorance of its true identity.

Arjuna begins this chapter by asking how he could possibly fight for his own selfish purposes, yet link with God and free himself from karma. Lord Krishna directs Arjuna to fight, but without attachment. If Arjuna simply sits down and renounces the fight, he will still be subject to his karma. But if he does his duty, not for his own sake but for God's pleasure, he will be practicing *karma-yoga*.

Work in *karma-yoga* is free from any sinful reaction, even if such work means fighting in the upcoming war. To further explain *karma-yoga*, Krishna points out that He has created both man and the gods. Man relates to the gods through prescribed duty and sacrifice, and the gods reward man with all the necessities of life.

Although unencumbered by any duty, Krishna works anyway, just to set a good example. To encourage Arjuna to do his duty, Krishna cites the example of the ancient king Janaka, an emblem of duty and sacrifice.

Neglect of duty, Krishna warns, leads to chaos. Those who understand the soul and karma generally work to educate others. Krishna directs the enlightened to teach where possible, but not to disturb those who have no interest. At the same time, Krishna emphasizes that everyone's duty is unique. Regardless of what one's duty may be, one must perform it without attachment.

At the chapter's end, Arjuna asks what drives one to sinful, karma-producing actions, even against one's will. In reply,

Lord Krishna elaborates on the yogic principles of sense control introduced in Chapter Two.

In this chapter, as in other places in the *Bhagavad-gita*, Lord Krishna refers to God in the third person. This in no way compromises Lord Krishna's many conclusive statements about His own supreme divinity. For instance, if the prime minister discusses the powers of the prime minister, he is talking about himself, but indirectly. Similarly, Lord Krishna speaks general theology to Arjuna. When Arjuna is ready for full enlightenment, he will know that the Supreme is Lord Krishna, as we shall see in later chapters.

Chapter 4: Knowledge Through the Disciplic Line

Having urged Arjuna to conquer lust, the foe of learning, Lord Krishna now reveals how to acquire spiritual knowledge. Actual, transformational spiritual knowledge comes through disciplic succession, a chain of gurus and disciples. Lord Krishna inaugurated the disciplic succession at the inception of the universe. Although time has broken the chain, Lord Krishna pledges to revive it with fresh, though unchanged, instructions to Arjuna.

Here, for the first time in the *Bhagavad-gita*, Lord Krishna clearly distinguishes Himself from ordinary souls. He points out that, while He remembers past lifetimes, Arjuna has forgotten them. Unlike ordinary souls, karma does not impose birth and death on Lord Krishna; He appears for His own reasons.

Lord Krishna then says that materialists disregard Him and worship the gods. He says that He reciprocates with everyone according to their surrender, and that to accommodate all types of people, He creates four social divisions. Our qualities and actions reveal to which division we each belong. (The subject of social divisions is further described in Chapter 18). Krishna declares that knowing these truths about Him will lead Arjuna to knowledge, as it has for past saints. Next, Krishna differentiates between actions for sense gratification, which produce karma, and transcendental actions, which don't. Transcendentalists act to please God, and God accepts such offerings of work. The transcendentalist thus enjoys a fully spiritualized life on earth and then returns to the kingdom of God.

In verses 25 through 33 Lord Krishna describes how various yogis approach the Absolute Truth. In verse 34 He advises Arjuna to find an expert guru who understands these paths and has himself realized their conclusion. Completing the chapter, Lord Krishna describes the beauty and power of transcendental knowledge and exhorts Arjuna to fight on and slay his ignorance.

Chapter 5: Acting in Consciousness of Krishna

Arjuna is again confused. At the end of Chapter Four, Lord Krishna advocates knowledge and renunciation, then again urges Arjuna to fight. Arjuna requests clear direction: should he renounce everything, or should he fight on behalf of God?

Explaining *karma-yoga* in even more detail, Krishna replies that both methods are acceptable, but acting for Him is better. By contrasting the self-serving work of a materialist and the work of a devotee, Krishna demonstrates how sacrificing one's work for God leads to sense control and freedom from karma.

Action in consciousness of Lord Krishna leads to enlightenment and happiness within the "city of nine gates"— the physical body, with its nine openings. Situated in realization, the master of the city sees the modes of nature at work within himself and others around him.

An enlightened soul sees all others equally, regardless of their position. Such a person avoids all kinds of problems by subduing the senses and thus relishes a higher happiness coming from within. This realization, the perfection of mysticism, leads to compassion for others still controlled by their senses.

In summary, Lord Krishna declares Himself to be the supreme proprietor, the supreme beneficiary of all work, and the supreme friend of every living being. He promises peace for anyone who knows Him in this way.

Chapter 6: Meditation and Mystic Yoga

Throughout the *Bhagavad-gita* Lord Krishna presents a variety of options to address Arjuna's perplexity. In this chapter Lord Krishna elaborates on the processes of meditation and mystic yoga, which He introduced briefly at the end of Chapter Five.

The successful yogi enjoys a profound equilibrium of mind and utter detachment from any external circumstance. To achieve this end, the mystic yogi must live in the forest, be celibate, reduce eating and sleeping to the bare minimum, and meditate constantly. In such meditation, the yogi repeatedly drags the wandering mind back to the task at hand.

After hearing this description, Arjuna objects that the mind is too difficult to control. Even after Lord Krishna reassures him, Arjuna still doubts his ability to succeed. Krishna then explains that a yogi benefits by simply trying. Lord Krishna concludes His account of this difficult yoga system by declaring that one who simply worships Him with faith is, in fact, the best of all yogis.

Chapter 7: Absolute Knowledge

Having identified the best yogi as one who serves and thinks of Him, Lord Krishna now explains how to attain such constant remembrance. During this explanation, Lord Krishna contrasts matter and spirit, evil and piety, and folly and wisdom. Matter, Lord Krishna's inferior energy, consists of eight basic elements: earth, water, air, fire, ether, mind, intelligence, and false ego. Ether refers to the subtle substance that allows radio waves to travel through space. False ego describes more than pride; it is the spiritual soul's misidentification with the material body.

Matter influences the conditioned soul as the three modes of nature (goodness, passion, and ignorance). Spirit—Lord Krishna's superior energy—consists of living beings struggling hard with the elements and modes of material nature.

Having introduced Himself as the origin of both matter and spirit, Lord Krishna describes metaphorically how one can see Him in matter. He then explains how to perceive Him directly through voluntary, loving submission.

Lord Krishna next describes four kinds of pious people who surrender to Him and four kinds of evil persons who do not. Among those who surrender, He expresses special appreciation for those who do so out of wisdom. Such intelligent persons, fortified with past pious deeds, take shelter of Krishna and transcend birth and death. On the other hand, fools worship gods for material gain—a popular custom among those who only casually follow the *Vedas*. Fools also consider that Lord Krishna has come from Brahman, a formless, impersonal energy. Such persons never know Lord Krishna, because for them He remains covered.

Chapter 8: Matter and Death, Soul and Supersoul

This chapter opens with several questions and answers that comprise most of the basic subjects of the *Bhagavad-gita*.
(1) What is Brahman?

Lord Krishna defines Brahman as the deathless soul. In the philosophy of Vaisnavism or devotion to Krishna, the individual soul is pure spirit, in quality one with Krishna. In quantity, however, the individual is vastly inferior to Krishna. A drop of ocean water may possess the qualities of water present throughout the entire the ocean, but a drop cannot sustain a boat. In the same way, individual souls are both one with and different from Lord Krishna, the Parabrahman, or Supreme Brahman.
(2) What is the material world?

Lord Krishna describes material creation as the ever-changing physical nature. By contrast, the spiritual nature, or Brahman, never changes.
(3) What is the self?

Lord Krishna refers to the self as the eternal nature of the soul. By nature, the soul serves; either he serves the physical creation and remains entangled, or he serves the spiritual creation and goes there. The entity who executes this free will is the self.

(4) What is karma?

Karma is the interaction of the changeless soul with the ever-mutating physical creation. The soul creates that interaction by choosing to serve matter, resulting in various physical bodies encapsulating the spiritual soul.

(5) Who are the gods?

The gods, highly elevated living beings, assist in the management of the physical creation. Under Lord Krishna's direction, they manipulate the weather, the planets, and everything else, including the mechanics of karma. They are components of Lord Krishna's vast universal form, as He reveals to Arjuna in Chapter Eleven.

Lord Krishna describes the life of Brahma, a chief god and the first created being in the universe. At the dawn of Brahma's vast daytime, the hosts of individual souls enter material bodies according to their karma. In his night-time, the souls return to an unmanifest condition. Eventually even Brahma dies. Lord Krishna then declares His own abode to be above the painful cycles of birth and death, creation and devastation.

(6) Who is the Lord of sacrifice?

The Lord or beneficiary of sacrifice is Lord Krishna, who dwells in the heart of every embodied being as the Supersoul.

(7) How can a devotee know Lord Krishna at the time of death?

Among Arjuna's questions in this chapter, Krishna speaks most about this, the destination of the soul. The state of mind one has at death, Krishna says, determines what kind of body one will attain in the next lifetime. Krishna then tells Arjuna how to think of Him and thus go to Him at death. Krishna goes on to discuss the mechanical methods of yoga, which help improve the soul's destination. But Krishna assures Arjuna that a devotee who thinks of Him doesn't have to worry about such mechanical considerations.

In conclusion, Lord Krishna declares that simply by being a *bhakta*, or devotee, one obtains the results of every kind of meritorious action.

Chapter 9: God's Personality

As the *Bhagavad-gita* progresses, Lord Krishna reveals His mind more intimately to Arjuna. In this chapter, after a formal description of His relationship with the material creation, Lord Krishna discloses His loving relationship with His devotees. Further explaining His divinity, Krishna states that He creates and pervades everything, yet remains a distinct and detached individual. Because conditioned souls stay engrossed in material energy, they cannot understand Krishna, even if they see Him. As a result, their plans fail. On the other hand, by knowing Krishna, the liberated souls become enlightened.

Lord Krishna then lists several ways to see Him, as He did in Chapter Seven. He again brings up the theme of misdirected worship. Pursuing extreme material happiness, some Vedic followers worship gods. Although after much effort such worshipers may attain heavenly bliss, they soon return to ordinary birth and death.

Lord Krishna closes the chapter with details of how a tiny individual soul enters a loving exchange with Him. Being a person, Lord Krishna enjoys a simple, affectionate offering of water, fruit, or flowers. He declares Himself impartial to everyone, yet He admits reciprocating in friendship with His devotee by relieving the devotee of all karma.

Chapter 10: Seeing and Serving God

Lord Krishna has advised Arjuna to become His devotee. Now Krishna tells him how to do so. Great commentators consider verses 8 through 11 of this chapter the essence of the *Bhagavad-gita*. In these four seminal verses, Lord Krishna describes how His devotees think of Him and enjoy a relationship with Him.

Arjuna then asks how he should think of Lord Krishna, and Krishna devotes the rest of the chapter to answering this question. He says that He can be perceived in the best and most powerful of every creation. Among stars He is the moon; among fish, the shark. After listing many such comparisons, Lord Krishna reminds Arjuna that whatever one can perceive with material senses reflects just the inferior, material portion of His creation.

Chapter 11: The Terrifying Cosmic Form of God

Pleased to hear of Lord Krishna's presence in so many ways, Arjuna now asks Krishna to show His feature known as the universal form, consisting of the entire material creation. Since the material universe comes from Lord Krishna, it is yet another one of His forms.

Krishna endows Arjuna with divine eyes to view this unprecedented display.

A dazzling vision suddenly overwhelms Arjuna. The brilliant, powerful radiance frightens him as it threatens to burn the whole creation. Arjuna grows terrified as the mouth of the universal form—the omnipotent crush of death—consumes the assembled warriors and everyone else. Arjuna cries, "Who are You?" Lord Krishna's answer (verse 11.32) is the famous *Bhagavad-gita* verse quoted by scientist Robert Oppenheimer as he watched the explosion of the first atomic bomb in the deserts of New Mexico: "Time I am, the great destroyer of the worlds. . . ."

Having seen Lord Krishna's limitless, deadly power, Arjuna understands his intimate friend in a new light. He apologizes for being too familiar in the past and begs to see again the friendly form of Lord Krishna. As Krishna reappears in His original form, He assures Arjuna that qualified people can always know Him in this more pleasing way.

Chapter 12: Loving God

Lord Krishna's universal form filled Arjuna with awe and fear, but Krishna prefers the love of His devotees. So in this chapter, the shortest in the *Bhagavad-gita*, Lord Krishna elaborates on the theme begun at the end of Chapter Eleven: *bhakti-yoga*, or personal devotional service to Him. Lord Krishna makes this point just after showing His universal form lest Arjuna, or anyone else, mistake the fearsome universal form for His ultimate manifestation.

The chapter begins with Arjuna asking about the comparative value of *bhakti-yoga* and realization of Brahman, Lord Krishna's impersonal feature. Krishna calls the Brahman path valid but difficult, while promising to personally deliver the faithful *bhakta*.

Lord Krishna then evaluates various practices of spiritual life. He declares that thinking of Him spontaneously, out of love, is best. For those who lack such love, practice of regulated *bhakti-yoga* ranks next. For those who decline *bhakti*, working for Lord Krishna is next, followed by working for some charitable cause. Krishna concludes the chapter by describing the many desirable qualities of His loving devotee.

Chapter 13: The Field and Its Knower

This chapter, which begins the final third of the *Bhagavad-gita*, is dedicated to *gyana-yoga*, or knowledge of God that leads one to serve Him. Arjuna asks about the body, the soul, the Supersoul, and the meaning and object of knowledge. Lord Krishna refers Arjuna to the *Vedanta-sutra*, an essential Vedic text, for a full explanation of the soul and matter. He then provides His own summary.

Krishna explains that both the soul and the Supersoul occupy the body, a vehicle made of dull matter. The soul knows only his body, but the Supersoul sits in every heart and knows everyone's pains and pleasures. While pursuing his illusory hope to enjoy matter, the soul encounters endless varieties of bodies and suffers and enjoys through them all. The Supersoul accompanies the soul on this painful journey. Lord Krishna concludes that those who learn the truth of their situation attain freedom from bondage to matter.

Chapter 14: Surpassing the Three Modes

Lord Krishna has just explained that matter entangles the soul and causes it to suffer. Now He elaborates. Matter exerts control over the soul through three qualities or modes: goodness, passion, and ignorance. Krishna often referred to the three modes in earlier chapters. In this chapter He explains them in detail. More discussion of the modes follows in Chapters Seventeen and Eighteen.

Lord Krishna first identifies Himself as the father of all living beings. He then defines the general characteristics of the three modes and their relationship with the soul. Actions in each of the modes create different results, both immediately and in future lifetimes. Krishna advises Arjuna to transcend the modes.

Arjuna asks how one can transcend the modes, and how to know a person who has done so. Lord Krishna answers both questions and concludes the chapter by declaring Himself to be the basis of all spiritual existence, beyond the modes.

Chapter 15: Supreme Personal Yoga

Lord Krishna begins this chapter with a metaphor, comparing the material world to a banyan tree. In India and other tropical countries, banyans grow to enormous sizes. They drop roots from their branches, and the roots form new trunks with new branches and roots. Thus banyans sometimes fill acres, and finding where they begin or end can be very difficult.

The metaphorical banyan has roots going up and branches going down. Such a tree exists only in a reflection, as in a lake. One reaching for an apple on such a reflected tree will end up with nothing but a wet arm.

Similarly, the material world reflects the spiritual world, capturing its shape and color but not its substance. The soul's natural love for God becomes misdirected and caught up in the temporary leaves and branches of this reflected material tree. Lord Krishna advises Arjuna to cut his relationship with it. After making such a cut, Lord Krishna says, one attains His abode.

Unlike the dark material universe, light prevails in Krishna's abode without the help of sun or electricity. Those infatuated with the material world miss the chance to return to the spiritual world. Nature forces such persons to take birth again.

As stated earlier, detachment from matter and attachment to Lord Krishna are one and the same. Thus, for Arjuna's benefit, Krishna again describes Himself. In verse 15 Krishna specifically describes His intimate relationship with each soul, as well as His presence in scriptures. Concluding the chapter, Krishna declares that knowing Him engages one in yoga of the Supreme Person.

Chapter 16: The Divine and the Demonic

At the beginning of the *Bhagavad-gita*, Lord Krishna distinguished the soul from the body. He then introduced the modes of nature and their various effects on the embodied souls. At Arjuna's request, He explained how to transcend the modes of nature. Now He describes the actions of a person under the lower modes—the lower branches of Chapter

Fifteen's banyan tree—as opposed to the actions of one who has transcended the three modes.

After summarizing the divine qualities belonging to those who have surpassed even the mode of goodness, Lord Krishna details the qualities of demons, who act only out of passion and ignorance. Filth, pride, atheism, dishonest action, and preoccupation with sexual enjoyment characterize such persons. Their wrong-headed perspective leads them to build horrible, destructive weapons. They aspire only to gratify their senses, and yet they make a show of charity and piety. In the end, they revile and make a mockery of true religion.

Lord Krishna describes their destination as the hell of life in subhuman species. A sane person thus gives up lust, anger, and greed—the three gates to hell. Abiding by the scriptures, such a person avoids the fate of demons.

Chapter 17: Faith, Food, and Sacrifice

After learning the fate of both followers and detractors of the scriptures, Arjuna now wants to know about persons who worship God without reference to the scriptures. Such persons have faith, but lacking scriptural basis, they may worship men or gods. Arjuna wants to know their destination.

Lord Krishna answers that faith not guided by scripture is another product of the three modes of nature. The modes influence how one eats, worships, and performs sacrifice, penance, and charity. After detailing all these activities in the different modes, Lord Krishna explains the transcendental approach. By directing to the Supreme Lord any sacrifice, penance, or charity, one rises above the influence of the modes of nature. Learned souls thus begin any sacrifice by chanting *om tat sat*, referring to the Supreme Absolute Truth. Reciting any name of the Supreme Lord has the same effect.

Lord Krishna concludes that anything done without an effort to please the Supreme is but the worthless floundering of a conditioned soul.

Chapter 18: Breaking the Bonds of Matter

This chapter, the longest in the *Bhagavad-gita*, summarizes the teachings of the entire text. Arjuna has just heard about the effects of the three modes of nature and the importance of directing one's work toward God. Lord Krishna rejected his superficial plan to renounce by leaving the battlefield. Now Arjuna asks how to truly renounce worldly affairs and dedicate his work to the Lord's service.

Lord Krishna analyzes renunciation according to goodness, passion, and ignorance. Although Krishna applauds detachment from the fruits of work, He specifies that no one benefits by renouncing sacrifice, charity, and penance. To show Arjuna why renunciation makes sense, Lord Krishna identifies five factors—mostly beyond Arjuna's control—that determine the result of any action. He goes on to evaluate action, the actor, knowledge, determination, understanding, and happiness, all according to the three modes of nature. In summary, Krishna declares that no one in the universe is exempt from the influence of the modes.

To clarify the influence of the modes on human society, Lord Krishna describes the system of *varnasrama*, or enlightened social organization. *Brahmanas* (priests) are in the mode of goodness, *ksatriyas* (warriors) in passion, *vaisyas* (farmers and merchants) in mixed passion and ignorance, and *sudras* (workers) in ignorance. *Varnasrama* designations are determined by inclination, not by birth (as in the caste system of India today). Although people have different inclinations, by pursuing renunciation through service to Lord Krishna, anyone can become perfect. Krishna explains exactly how this can be done and the symptoms of one who has done it.

Lord Krishna now begins to conclude the *Bhagavad-gita* by declaring that His servant will come to Him and be protected under all circumstances. He bluntly tells Arjuna that giving up on the battle would be the wrong kind of renunciation and that Arjuna's nature would force him to fight anyway. Advising complete surrender to His will and promising all protection, Lord Krishna at last tells Arjuna to choose his course of action.

Krishna has described numerous options for Arjuna. He has outlined the paths of piety, mystic yoga, and *gyana* (knowledge). Through them all, He has consistently emphasized the paramount importance of Arjuna's fighting as an expression of surrender to Him. Although Krishna has also declared and displayed His omnipotent divinity, He concludes by telling Arjuna that the choices are now his. After blessing the speakers and hearers of *Bhagavad-gita*, Krishna asks Arjuna if his illusions are now gone.

Arjuna emphatically answers, "Yes!" Through the course of the *Bhagavad-gita*, Arjuna has gone from confidence to depression, curiosity to enlightenment, admiration to fear, and finally from love and wisdom to realization.

Sanjaya, the visionary narrator, concludes the *Bhagavad-gita* with expressions of personal gratitude and ecstasy. In his rapture, he spontaneously discloses the harsh truth of the battle's outcome to his blind master, Dhritarashtra.

Appendices

Sample Verse

To show the origin of the verses you're reading in this edition of *Bhagavad-gita*, here is a sample text taken from start to finish —the original Devanagari text, Prabhupada's word-for-word translation, Prabhupada's complete English translation, and my poetic rendition.

VERSE 15.12

yad āditya-gatam tejo
jagad bhāsayate 'khilam
yac candramasi yac cāgnau
tat tejo viddhi māmakam

SYNONYMS

yat—that which; *āditya-gatam*—in the sunshine; *tejaḥ*—splendor; *jagat*—the whole world; *bhāsayate*—illuminates; *akhilam*—entirely; *yat*—that which; *candramasi*—in the moon; *yat*—that which; *ca*—also; *agnau*—in fire; *tat*—that; *tejaḥ*—splendor; *viddhi*—understand; *māmakam*—from Me.

TRANSLATION

The splendor of the sun, which dissipates the darkness of this whole world, comes from Me. And the splendor of the moon and the splendor of fire are also from Me.

POETIC RENDITION

Scattering the darkness that encircles everyone,
I create the brilliant fire, the splendid moon and sun.

Mantra Page

As taught by Sri Caitanya Mahaprabhu, in the present age of anxiety and quarrel, the simplest way to meditate is known as mantra meditation, or chanting names of God. This chanting may be done individually or in a group. There are no hard and fast rules for chanting. Although the process works with any name of God in any language, many Sanskrit names of God are commonly chanted, such as Krishna, Rama, Govinda, Nrsimha, and thousands of others. These are some of the most common mantras chanted by Vaishnavas (devotees of Krishna):

> Govinda Jaya Jaya, Gopala Jaya Jaya
> Radha Ramana Hari, Govinda Jaya, Jaya

(All glories to Krishna, who pleases the cows, the cowherd boys, and Srimati Radharani.)

> Sita Rama, Jaya Sita Rama
> Sita Rama, Jaya Sita Rama

(All glories to Lord Ramachandra and Sita.)

> Hare Krishna Hare Krishna, Krishna Krishna Hare Hare
> Hare Rama Hare Rama, Rama Rama Hare Hare

(My dear Lord, please engage me in Your devotional service.)

Personalities in the *Bhagavad-gita*
(in order of appearance)

Dhritarashtra [DRIT– tah – RASH – trah] – The aged blind king of the Kurus. Elder brother of the late King Pandu, his sons usurped the kingdom of Hastinapura from Pandu's sons by deceit. In the *Mahabharata*, Dhritarashtra wavers between doing the right thing and capitulating to his evil sons.

Sanjaya [sahn – JIYE – ah] – Dhritarashtra's secretary.

Duryodhana [duhr – YO – dhahn or duhr – YO – dhahn – ah] – Dhritarastra's oldest son and leader of the plots against the Pandavas.

Drona [DROW – nah]–The honorable military guru who taught the art of war to both the sons of Pandu and the sons of Dhritarashtra. Duryodhana manipulated things in such a way that Drona was obliged to fight for his side.

Bhisma [BEESH – mah] – Dhritarashtra's uncle and long-term caretaker of the kingdom. Bhisma, a lifetime celibate, was the beloved elder statesman of the kingdom who, like Drona, was forced by Duryodhana to fight against the Pandavas. Throughout the conflict, Duryodhana repeatedly failed to heed Bhisma's good advice, resulting in disaster for the Kurus.

Arjuna [ahr – JOON – ah or ahr-JOON] – The third of the five Pandava sons. Arjuna was an unparalleled archer and Drona's favorite student.

Krishna – The Supreme Personality of Godhead serving as Arjuna's friend and chariot driver. Krishna appeared before the battle of Kurukshetra to help reduce the heavy military build-up on the earth. In the *Bhagavad-gita* the mystical Krishna identifies Himself as God, but because of His illusory energy, few people knew it.

BHAGAVAD-GITA AS IT IS

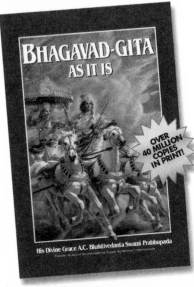

By His Divine Grace A.C. Bhaktivedanta Swami Prabhupada

The *Bhagavad-gita* is the concise summary of India's spiritual teachings. Remarkably, the setting for this classic is a battlefield. Just before the battle, the great warrior Arjuna begins to inquire from Lord Krishna about the meaning of life. The *Gita* systematically guides one along the path of self-realization. It is the main source book for information on karma, reincarnation, yoga, devotion, the soul, Lord Krishna, and spiritual enlightenment. *Bhagavad-gita As It Is* is the best-selling edition in the world!

> "*Bhagavad-gita As It Is* is a deeply felt, powerfully conceived, and beautifully explained work. I have never seen any other work on the *Gita* with such an important voice and style. It is a work of undoubted integrity. It will occupy a significant place in the intellectual and ethical life of modern man for a long time to come." —Dr. Shaligram Shukla, Assistant Professor of Linguistics, Georgetown University

Deluxe edition with translations and elaborate purports:
$24.95 ♦ ISBN 0-89213-285-X ♦ 6.5" x 9.5"
♦ Hardbound ♦ 1068 pgs. ♦ 29 full-color plates
Standard edition, including translations and elaborate purports:
$12.95 ♦ ISBN 0-89213-123-3 ♦ 5.5" x 8.5"
♦ Hardbound ♦ 924 pgs. ♦ 14 full-color plates

INTERACTIVE

BHAGAVAD-GITA AS IT IS

Produced by Krsna Prema Dasa and Nitya-trpta Devi Dasi

This is an excellent educational tool for all families who have a computer in the home, and a good reason to get one if you don't. The interactive CD has six main areas of interest, divided into subcategories. Presentation slides allow the viewer to read the text while music plays in the background, or the viewer can listen as the verses, purports, or essays are being read. Other sections include video clips to present the information.

The navigational tools are easy to understand and use, so any member of your family can easily find his or her way around the many areas of interest. Included on the CD is a VedaBase demo containing Srila Prabhupada's entire *Bhagavad-gita As It Is* and all his Gita lectures.

For Mac or PC CD- Rom, over 30 hours of Audio, 275 full-color illustrations, video clips, and nearly 1,000 pages of text.

$19.95
ISBN 91-7149-415-4

MAHABHARATA

The Greatest Spiritual Epic of All Time

As the divinely beautiful Draupadi rose from the fire, a voice rang out from the heavens foretelling a terrible destiny: "She will cause the destruction of countless warriors." And so begins one of the most fabulous stories of all time. *Mahabharata* plunges us into a wondrous and ancient world of romance and adventure. In this exciting new rendition of the renowned classic, Krishna Dharma condenses the epic into a fast-paced novel-a powerful and moving tale recounting the fascinating adventures of the five heroic Pandava brothers and their celestial wife. Culminating in an apocalyptic war, *Mahabharata* is a masterpiece of suspense, intrigue, and illuminating wisdom.

> "A well-wrought saga that will be appreciated by Western readers. Highly recommended."—*The Midwest Book Review*

> "...very readable, its tone elevated without being ponderous."—*Library Journal*

> "...blockbuster treatment...Moves effortlessly, often as racily as a thriller, without compromising the elevated style and diction."—*India Today*

> "Its truths are unassailable, its relevance beyond dispute, and its timelessness absolute."—*Atlantis Rising*

> "I could not tear my mind away!"—*Magical Blend*

Condensed Version
$19.95 ♦ ISBN 1-887089-25-X ♦ 6" x 9" ♦ Hardbound ♦ 288 pgs.
Complete Unabridged Version
$39.95 ♦ ISBN 1-887089-17-9 ♦ 6" x 9" ♦ Hardbound ♦ 960 pgs.
♦ 16 color plates ♦ 20 Illustrations

Book Order Form

- ◆ Telephone orders: Call 1-888-TORCHLT (1-888-867-2458)
    (Please have your credit card ready.)
- ◆ Fax orders: 559-337-2354
- ◆ Postal Orders: Torchlight Publishing, P.O. Box 52,
    Badger, CA 93603, USA   🌐 www.torchlight.com

PLEASE SEND THE FOLLOWING:	QUANTITY	AMOUNT

☐Bhagavad-gita As It Is
Deluxe (1,068 pages)—$24.95   x_____ = $_____
Standard (924 pages)—$12.95   x_____ = $_____
☐Bhagavad-gita Interactive CD—$19.95   x_____ = $_____
☐Bhagavad-gita, The Song Divine—$15.00 x_____ = $_____
☐Mahabharata, Condensed—$19.95   x_____ = $_____
☐Mahabharata, Unabridged—$39.95   x_____ = $_____
Shipping/handling (see below) . . . .$_____
Sales tax 7.25% (California only) . . . .$_____
   TOTAL . . . .$_____
(I understand that I may return any book for a full refund—no questions asked.)

☐ PLEASE SEND YOUR CATALOG AND INFO ON OTHER BOOKS BY TORCHLIGHT PUBLISHING

Company _____

Name _____

Address _____

City _____ State _____ Zip _____

PAYMENT:

☐ Check/money order enclosed   ☐ VISA ☐ MasterCard ☐ American Express

Card number _____

Name on card _____ Exp. date _____

Signature _____

SHIPPING AND HANDLING:

USA: $4.00 for the first book and $3.00 for each additional book.
Airmail per book (USA only)—$7.00.
Canada: $6.00 for the first book and $3.50 for each additional book.
(NOTE: Please allow 3 to 4 weeks for delivery in North America.)
Foreign countries: $8.00 for the first book and $5.00 for each additional
book. Please allow 6 to 8 weeks for delivery.